The KABBALAH CODE

Also by James F. Twyman

Books

The Art of Spiritual Peacemaking: *Secret Teachings from Jeshua ben Joseph*
Emissary of Light
Emissary of Love: *The Psychic Children Speak to the World*
Messages from Thomas: *Raising Psychic Children*
The Moses Code: *The Most Powerful Manifestation Tool in the History of the World**
The Prayer of St. Francis
Praying Peace: *In Conversation with Gregg Braden and Doreen Virtue*
The Proposing Tree: *A Love Story*
The Secret of the Beloved Disciple
Ten Spiritual Lessons I Learned at the Mall

Films

Indigo: *A Film of Faith, Family, and an Extraordinary Child*
The Indigo Evolution
Into Me See
The Moses Code: *The Movie**

Music

Ecclesia: *Volume One*
Emissary of Light: *Songs from the Peace Concerts*
For the Beloved: *An Intimate Evening with James Twyman*
God Has No Religion
May Peace Prevail on Earth
The Moses Code Frequency Meditation*
The Order of the Beloved Disciple

*Available from Hay House

Please visit Hay House USA: **www.hayhouse.com**®
Hay House Australia: **www.hayhouse.com.au**
Hay House UK: **www.hayhouse.co.uk**
Hay House South Africa: **www.hayhouse.co.za**
Hay House India: **www.hayhouse.co.in**

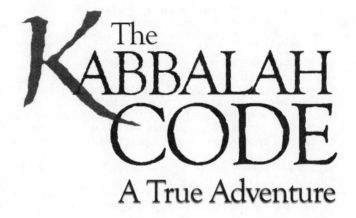

The KABBALAH CODE

A True Adventure

James F. Twyman

with Philip Gruber

HAY HOUSE, INC.
Carlsbad, California • New York City
London • Sydney • Johannesburg
Vancouver • Hong Kong • New Delhi

Published and distributed in the United States by: Hay House, Inc.: www
.hayhouse.com • *Published and distributed in Australia by:* Hay House
Australia Pty. Ltd.: www.hayhouse.com.au • *Published and distributed in the
United Kingdom by:* Hay House UK, Ltd.: www.hayhouse.co.uk • *Published and
distributed in the Republic of South Africa by:* Hay House SA (Pty), Ltd.: www
.hayhouse.co.za • *Distributed in Canada by:* Raincoast: www.raincoast.com
Published in India by: Hay House Publishers India: www.hayhouse.co.in

Editorial supervision: Jill Kramer • *Design:* Amy Gingery

Library of Congress Cataloging-in-Publication Data

Twyman, James F.
  The Kabbalah code : a true adventure / James F. Twyman ; with Philip Gruber.
-- 1st ed.
      p. cm.
  ISBN 978-1-4019-2404-1 (hardcover : alk. paper) 1. Cabala--Miscellanea. I.
Gruber, Philip. II. Title.
  BF1623.C2T89 2009
  299'.93--dc22
                              2008047371

ISBN: 978-1-4019-2404-1

12 11 10 09   4 3 2 1
1st edition, May 2009

Printed in the United States of America

To Debbie Ford and Andrew Harvey.
Your love and support have taught me more than words
can express, and you have also pushed me in ways that
have helped me grow. I am eternally grateful for every part
of the journey we've shared.

Contents

Introduction

The greatest lessons we learn usually come through the adventures that shape and change our lives. This adventure, the one I describe in this book, came upon me as a great surprise. I didn't set out to do any of the things you're about to read, nor did I initially think that they would result in a book that others might find valuable. But the more I sat with it and reflected on the details of those two amazing days in April 2008, the more I realized that this adventure wasn't meant for Phil and me alone. It was nice having a partner in the journey—someone to not only share the remarkable details with, but to also verify them later. A witness is a good thing to have when recounting something so extraordinary.

As stated on the front cover, this is a true story, but for some that may be hard to believe. I'm lucky to have traveled around the world as a Peace Troubadour and to have had many such adventures, but there still may be those who read these words and think, *Come on, did that really happen?* The answer is *yes*, but as much as I want it to be that simple, it isn't. Many of the events that took place and which I describe are subjective in nature, meaning that they were my own personal experiences. If you were there with us, you may have had a different experience altogether, but that's the way things usually are.

Many of us have heard this famous example: five people witness the same car accident but report the details in completely different manners. It's human nature. But there's also a deeper truth, and that is what I'm more interested in portraying here. A number of the experiences you're about to read will seem amazing and perhaps even unbelievable, but the truth behind them all is the same: we currently have the opportunity to use this universal wisdom to change the world and inspire lasting peace. The only question that remains is, *Will we accept the challenge?*

I met Phil Gruber 12 years ago and have called upon him many times for support and wisdom. Since then he has developed his own audience—people who, like me, have realized the scope and importance of his vast knowledge and profound intellect. It's hard to say what his special focus may be since he seems to know a great deal about any spiritual topic one might mention. If you were to ask for a spiritual dissertation on the historical importance of the Knights Templar, he would be able to lecture for days, or if you wanted to know more about the varied incarnations of the Divine Feminine throughout the last 300 years, it would be the same. To say that he is an interesting character would be an understatement. His sense of humor is infectious, and his grasp of spiritual matters is profound, but it's his friendship that has meant the most to me.

I was concerned when I heard that he'd endured another serious bout of depression and almost hesitated calling him for his thoughts on some puzzling questions I was presented with (which I describe in the first chapter). However, as soon as I mentioned my dilemma, he shot into action, and you're about to read the results. From the moment Phil showed up in Geneva to the final conclusion of this story in Paris, he was instrumental in orchestrating one of the most incredible experiences of my life. I also hope that you'll enjoy getting to know him in these pages as much as I've enjoyed having him in my life. Without Phil, none of it would have been possible.

Kabbalism is the mystical path of Judaism most recently made popular by some of its famous adherents, including Madonna and other celebrities. I've known about it for many years, but to be honest, I never felt an attraction to explore Kabbalah for myself because it seemed to be so centered on the intellect and other mental constructs. I couldn't have been more wrong. Although a comprehensive study would be enough to set anyone's brain spinning, there is an experiential depth that I didn't expect.

In my last book, *The Moses Code,* I wrote about the first name of God that was given to Moses at the burning bush 3,500 years ago—"Ehyeh Asher Ehyeh." At the time, I didn't know that I was treading on several major Kabbalistic themes (and not always gently). It wasn't until I was publicly called out on my ignorance that a new exploration began, one that led to the writing of this book. I may still be a complete novice when it comes to the subject, but I believe I'm a bit wiser and a great deal more experienced.

So relax, and get ready for a story that may change your life. At the very least, it will unlock doors and reveal hidden treasures you may not have even known you've had. I do know that the ancient teachings of Kabbalah are as important today as they've ever been, and this story may be a first step toward understanding its vast implications. I don't claim to be an authority in this rich science, as you'll soon discover, but at least I've had the chance to peek inside the temple. That's all it took to hook me for life.

— **James F. Twyman**

✧✧✧✧✧

CHAPTER 1

The Moses Code

The world premiere of *The Moses Code,* the film based on my book of the same name, was to be a momentous occasion. Liz Dawn, one of the owners of Mishka Productions, didn't think that I'd given her enough time to gather a large crowd. I called her two and a half weeks earlier with the idea of launching the documentary in Scottsdale, Arizona, a couple of weeks before it would open in theaters and venues around the world. To her, it was an impossibly small amount of time to organize anything close to what I wanted, but I had a good feeling and knew it would be a triumph. I'd been working on the film for over a year and was anxious to see the final version in front of a real audience. I assured Liz that if she promoted the event, the audience would come, and I was right. More than 600 people crammed into the conference hall that night, and I could hear the buzz of excitement as I walked through the crowd moments before the lights dimmed and the movie began.

"James, can I talk to you?"

I recognized the man's face, but his name floated just beyond my reach. After 12 years of traveling around the world promoting books and movies and performing peace concerts in some of the most war-torn countries on Earth, specific names were sometimes hard to summon. Faces were a different story, though, and I knew that if I could get him talking, before long his name would come back to me.

"Hi," I said to him, holding my hand out. "How are you?"

"Fantastic, man. I was so excited to hear you were opening the new movie here."

He was young, perhaps 30, and I was sure we'd met before, perhaps several times. The harder I tried to recall him, the further the memory receded into the back of my brain. My eyes must have betrayed the confusion I felt.

"Mike," he said, unsurprised. "Mike Larson. I attended a workshop you did at a Celebrate Your Life conference about two years ago. We spoke afterward . . . I don't remember exactly what we discussed."

"Neither do I," I remarked, trying to regain control. I was attempting to make my way to the front of the room so we could begin the screening. "I do remember your face, though, even after two years. That's not too bad."

"Not at all," he said without letting go of my hand. "I can't wait to see this movie. I saw the trailer online, and it looked incredible . . . just what the world needs."

"What the world needs?"

"You know, after *The Secret* and everything. I think this film is going to be the next step. I'll let you know after I see it."

I used my left hand to pry free the one locked in his grip without him realizing it. It was a skill I'd learned over the years—how to politely end a conversation without the other person noticing the shift. It came in handy in situations like this one. "I hope I see you afterward," I said to him as I began walking away. "I'd love to hear what you think."

"I'll tell you the truth—that's for sure," he said over the shoulder of a dark-haired woman who just happened to be between us. "I'm sure someone like you needs to hear the truth."

The statement confused me, and I stopped. "I'm not sure I know what you mean," I said, walking back to him.

"You know . . . people usually say what they think you want to hear. I don't mean just you, but it wouldn't surprise me. You're the kind of person people want to impress, and that could be hard if they told you they didn't like a movie or a book or something else you did."

I could see him becoming uncomfortable in his own skin, as if he couldn't stop talking even though he knew nothing was coming out as he had intended.

"I know what you mean," I said, saving him further embarrassment. "Luckily, I have lots of people around me who are willing to be brutally honest. In fact, we probably wouldn't be here tonight if that weren't true."

"Really?"

"I spent a year working on the movie, and when I thought it was done, I showed it to a few friends. They told me the truth, even though it was kind of hard to hear. They said it was *okay,* but not great. Obviously, I didn't spend a year of my life just to make an average movie, so we went back to work despite the fact that we were already past our deadline. We spent two weeks tearing it apart, re-editing, and reshooting almost 75 percent of it."

"You did all that in two weeks?" he asked, amazed.

"You know," I said, beginning to walk toward the stage again, "I think that if we went into the reshoot knowing how much work was going to be involved, we wouldn't have done it. Sometimes you're better off not knowing what you're getting yourself into. It just sort of happened. All I can say is that it all started with a few friends telling me the truth, and luckily, I listened."

Liz had just climbed the stairs to the podium and was getting ready to start the evening. I made my way to the front and sat down, waiting for the microphone to go live and the audience to find their seats. It was finally time to see if all the work translated into a film that would not only be successfully received, but would also inspire people to change the world.

✧✧✧

The Moses Code was conceived as a book long before the idea came to make it into a film. I'd stumbled across the concept when

I was working on another book three years earlier—one that I consider to be my greatest accomplishment: *The Art of Spiritual Peacemaking.* As I was writing, a story I'd first heard as a child kept coming into focus; it was the story of Moses and how he secured the release of the Israelite slaves 3,500 years ago.

God appeared to Moses in the form of a burning bush and asked him to do the impossible: go to the Pharaoh, Ramses the Great, and tell him to let the Israelites leave and find the Promised Land. Moses, knowing the remarkable improbability of success, decided to ask God a question that no Israelite had ever asked before—he wanted to know God's name. Up to that point in religious history, the Israelites had no name for God. God was known simply as the "God of Abraham" or the "God of our forefathers." Moses knew that if he was going to accomplish the task, he'd need more information, something that would profoundly inspire his people. A name would do that, and God gave it to him.

The first name usually associated with this conversation is *Ehyeh Asher Ehyeh,* usually translated as "I AM THAT I AM." As a young child, and even as an adult, I heard the phrase spoken but never understood what it meant. And since I didn't comprehend it, I disregarded any importance it might have held. It's clear from the story, however, that the name contained great significance. The miracles that Moses produced, ultimately leading to the release of the Israelites, came about through his harnessing the power of God's name and effectively directing that power. I figured there was something I was missing—the knowledge that would allow me to finally comprehend one of the greatest mysteries in the history of the world. But what was it?

I was in Israel when the tumblers fell into place. While visiting the Dead Sea, I had an experience that resulted in my writing *The Art of Spiritual Peacemaking,* a large part of which involved Moses's conversation with God at the burning bush. I was meditating on the name I AM THAT I AM when suddenly it seemed to change. It would be more accurate to say that *I* changed, or that my perspective shifted gears, and something new (or very old) fell instantly into place—a comma.

As I watched the name of God in my mind, I saw a comma fall like a comet, landing right after the word *that*. The single sentence was now in two parts: I AM THAT, I AM. In the same instant, I also understood a mystery that had eluded me until then—the meaning of the name. This wasn't the indecipherable equation I thought it was, but rather a love letter from God to humanity with the secret for manifesting everything we desire. And that was only the first layer. Behind it there were other mysteries, deeper teachings that if understood would lead humankind into the direct experience of the Divine. This simple comma had unlocked the mystery behind the greatest gift God had ever given the world: the actual formula for creating miracles.

The words of *The Moses Code* flew out of me as if it had already been written. In some ways it was hard to believe that no one had realized this before I did. It seemed so simple, and yet every time I put it into practice, miracles followed. The subtitle I chose, "The Most Powerful Manifestation Tool in the History of the World," was a big statement, but the more I worked with the Code, the more I believed it was true.

The phrase I AM THAT can be found in many religions and esoteric traditions. It's a statement of sacred union, of seeing the Oneness within something that seems to be isolated and alone. This is what God was saying to Moses when he asked him to go to the Pharaoh: *I am that freedom*. And since we cannot be separated from our Divine Source, *we* are that freedom, too. It isn't something we want or hope to someday achieve. God is saying, *You are that already*.

It was the same power that Jesus harnessed throughout his three-year ministry. He said, "Before Abraham was, I AM." And because uttering the name of God was considered to be the highest blasphemy by the orthodoxy, the next line in the gospel says that people picked up rocks to stone him, such was the gravity of the offense. I could feel the same power as I sat down to write the book, and just as with Moses and Jesus, miracles began filling my life.

Then came the movie. The book was already written, and the rights had been sold to Hay House. Around the same time,

The Secret was released and began spreading its wings across the entire planet. Millions of people were suddenly turned on to the Law of Attraction, and the illusion was created that it had been hidden away by powerful forces. It may not have been true, but it certainly sparked massive devotion. Before long, *The Secret* was the highest-grossing spiritual film of all time, and it seemed that humanity had finally learned how to manifest a new world.

But it wasn't meant to be. Unfortunately, most of the information in *The Secret* was focused on using spiritual laws to get more things, such as cars, houses, and money. Very little energy went into balancing those desires with the wisdom of the soul, and so people were soon disenfranchised with the message and began throwing the baby out with the bathwater. The focus of *The Moses Code* was less about "getting"; instead, its focus was on giving everything. It dealt with what I like to call *soul manifestation,* creating from the longing of the soul rather than the ego. It was suggested that I take matters into my own hands and produce a movie that would pick up where *The Secret* left off. In the spring of 2007, I began production on *The Moses Code* movie, and the comma once again came into focus.

A year later, I was in Scottsdale for the premiere of the finished film. Some of the best-known spiritual teachers in the world agreed to be part of the project, and by the time we arrived in Arizona for the screening, the energy had grown to a fevered pitch. Everyone was waiting to see if the film would live up to the hype, and I was no different.

It was the first time seeing the film with an audience, hearing the laughs and watching all the pieces fall into place . . . hopefully. It couldn't have gone any better, though, and when the final credits began to roll, the entire crowd was on its feet, greeting us with wild applause.

After a moment, Liz and her assistants set microphones and chairs on the stage so I could answer questions and listen to remarks. This is always a moment I both crave and fear. It's a great gift to hear from an audience, especially when they liked the film. But on the other hand, if they didn't like it, then it would be a very different experience. In every crowd, there's also at least one naysayer who demands to be heard, and if the person's point is well presented and on the mark, the view of an entire crowd can be turned in a minute. As I sat down in the chair, I scanned the audience for any potential threats. For the most part, everyone I saw seemed happy and content, including the young woman in the front row who was determined to go first. I acknowledged her and asked if she had a question. It started off nice enough.

"First of all," she said, as she stood tall so everyone in the room could see her, "I want to commend you for a well-made film. I really feel that it will be successful and touch millions of people. But there's something else I want to mention."

She tipped her hand, and I knew she was heading off in a new direction. The fact that she was the very first person to speak wasn't a good sign. She would set the tone for the entire evening, and if she said something negative, it would be up to me to turn it around quickly . . . or else. A knot was beginning to form in my stomach as she continued.

"I'm Jewish, and I'm also a student of Kabbalah, the esoteric teachings of Judaism," she said. "And I have to say that I was deeply offended that you reduced God to a comma. For me, that was an outrage and a profound blow."

I could tell from her energy that she wasn't going to let this end gracefully, and I realized that I had to save things as quickly as possible. If I didn't find a way to make things right with her, then we were going to be in for a very long evening.

"I want to say that it wasn't our intention to reduce God to a comma," I said, interrupting her. "The comma was used as a device to unlock the deeper meaning in the name of God. If it came across in any other way, then I want you to know that it wasn't intended."

"You're not Jewish," she replied, not slowing down, "so I don't expect you to understand what I'm about to explain. Anyone who is Jewish knows that the comma looks very similar to the Yud, the smallest yet most important letter in the Hebrew alphabet. The Yud is the hand of God representing Divine energy flowing from

Heaven to Earth. I doubt you knew this, but it doesn't change the fact that you've stepped on one of the holiest truths in the Universe. It reminds me of Jesus when he said, 'Forgive them Lord, for they know not what they do.'"

I tried to interject, to say anything that would turn things back in my favor, but she wouldn't allow it. Even when members of the audience asked her to stop, it only added fuel to the fire.

"What would you have me do to correct this?" I finally asked. "And I'm still having a difficult time seeing why it's so offensive."

"I have no idea what you should do," she said, her growing anger reaching its apex. "And the fact that you can't see why it's offensive makes it even worse for me. Imagine me trampling on a Christian doctrine that you hold dear. It ruined the entire film for me, and that's really too bad because, otherwise, I liked it very much. But this I cannot condone."

By then the audience had heard enough and asked her to pass the microphone to someone else. Unable to contain her feelings, she handed it to the volunteer standing next to her and stormed out of the room. After taking a deep, cleansing breath, I tried to find someone with a kind face and open smile to go to next, but it really didn't matter. The question-and-answer session went on for another half hour, but it never really got on track.

As I walked out of the room when it was over, I saw Mike Larson.

"Hey man, nice film," he said with a smile. "I really mean it."

"Thanks. Hearing what people really feel seems to be what this night was all about, even if it wasn't always very easy or fun."

✧✧✧

Days later, I still hadn't shaken the uncomfortable feeling from that night. On the one hand, I was sorry that an otherwise perfect event had been turned against me, and yet there was something more, something that kept poking at my consciousness with unrelenting persistence. What if that woman had been right? Was my revelation about the comma in *The Moses Code* movie going to offend the very group that had inspired the entire project, both the book and the film? Would every Jewish person I met from that point on have the same reaction and accuse me of being shamelessly naïve? A dark cloud seemed to hang over what I had put so much love and effort into, and I wasn't sure what my next step should be.

There was another thought that drove me, one that was even more pressing than the opinion of other people. Of course, I'd never heard of the Yud before that night. If what the woman said was true, then there had to be a correlation between the comma I used to explain the Code and the smallest letter in the Hebrew alphabet. She mentioned the "hand of God," and that the Yud represented the flow of Divine Light to humanity, which sounded very much like the concept I developed with the Moses Code.

Manifestation only occurs when we link our being with the being of God. *The Secret* may have focused on ego manifestation—or the act of attracting stuff—but true manifestation comes from the soul, and the soul is the highest aspect of who we are. It's the part of us that is fully aligned with our Source, otherwise known as God. I started to wonder if this was more than a coincidence, and if the woman in Scottsdale wasn't actually a messenger.

I decided to do some research online and see what I could learn about the Yud. As the woman had stated, it's the smallest letter in the Hebrew alphabet and is said to represent the primal vibration of the Universe. The analogy of the hand of God comes from the Yud's shape, which has a tip extending upward and an appendage trailing downward like a traditional comma. The Yud is the hand that draws energy from Heaven and then anchors it on Earth. It's also been said that all other Hebrew letters sprang from the Yud. In fact, it's the only letter that is often placed above others because of its transcendent qualities. And because it is the smallest letter, it represents the *all* that is contained within the most diminutive thing. But there was something that was an even greater surprise.

The Yud is also known as an aspect of the Creative Fire, a fire that cannot be consumed. Images of Moses at the burning bush immediately filled my mind. Is it possible that when God appeared to Moses and first revealed the Holy Name, it was actually the energy of the Yud that Moses was experiencing? My initial inspiration of the Moses Code being a comma was beginning to make more and more sense.

About a week after I made these discoveries, I was scheduled to give a lecture at the Sivananda Ashram Yoga Retreat on Paradise Island in the Bahamas. I'd visited the ashram at least five times over the years and always loved the opportunity to be in the atmosphere, chanting and praying, and of course, sitting on the beach. It was just what I needed after so many concentrated months of work getting the movie finished and released.

The director of the ashram is named Swami Swaroopananda. Originally from Israel, he is one of the most intelligent men I've ever met, especially in matters of spirituality and spiritual practice. In addition, he had lived and worked directly with Swami Vishnu-devananda, the Indian master who brought Sivananda yoga to the West. One of the things that always impressed me about this organization is its dedication to peace, something that came from Vishnu-devananda himself. He was known as the Flying Yogi and often flew his single-engine airplane into dangerous situations to promote peace. He even flew over the Berlin Wall during the height of tensions there, despite being warned that his plane would be shot down if detected. Swami Swaroopananda had been part of organizing that flight and once shared the details with me. James Bond couldn't have been better prepared for a mission, and in the end, it was successful. This was the type of person I wanted to model myself after.

For several days I tried to get a meeting with Swami Swaroopananda, but his busy schedule made it difficult for him to break away. It wasn't until after I gave my talk on the Moses Code that he could finally meet with me.

"I didn't know anything about the Yud before that night in Scottsdale," I told him after I explained what happened at the premiere, "but ever since then, I've become obsessed with it. The connections are too amazing to be mere coincidence. It feels like I was led along only so far, and until now the only way I had to understand the Moses Code was to call it a comma. Now I see that it's much more than that. I'm starting to feel that this rabbit hole goes much deeper than I thought it did."

"There is no question about this," Swami remarked in his thick Israeli accent. We were sitting on hard wooden chairs next to the bay where the sound of passing boats made it hard to hear. "These are very deep mysteries, and it's clear to me that you're being guided by God."

"That's why I wanted to ask you about it," I continued. "Your experience with the Kabbalah could be very helpful. I just need to learn more. I feel that if I do, then I could solve this and finally understand everything."

"But there is nothing to solve, and you'll never understand it," he replied. "You're trying to do too much with your mind, but it isn't your mind that has brought you this far—it's your soul. You've been guided here through direct revelation, and that's the only way this can be understood. I could give you more information about the Yud and Kabbalah, but I'm afraid if I do, it might bring you more harm than good."

"How could that hurt me? Wouldn't it help me sort through everything I've already read?"

"I think it would only confuse you more, and that's something I don't want to happen," he answered, as he reached for his handkerchief and touched his forehead. "There is something I can tell you about the Kabbalah that may help you, though."

I sensed that I was about to receive what I came for. In the past, I felt like the Swami was always playing with me, testing me to see what he should say or how much information he should offer. His responses were often cloaked with intrigue, and I didn't expect this occasion to be any different. But this was the first time I felt desperate to learn from him. He was the only person I knew with such experience and knowledge, and I was determined to receive it.

"There are two types of Kabbalah," he said, leaning back in his seat. "The first is the one that is written down. This is not the true Kabbalah. The second is received through direct experience.

This is the true Kabbalah. Only that which is received through direct revelation can be said to be true. When you read a book or if I tell you what I know, then you're experiencing another person's interpretation of their direct revelation. This will only satisfy the mind, which is always seeking to avoid the true Kabbalah. It's clear to me that you've been guided to this point, and there's no reason for me to think that it will not continue. Therefore, I'm not going to tell you anything more because I want you to proceed exactly as you are now. The more you trust the way God is revealing everything, the more it will endure. Then you'll know everything you need to know, and the answers you seek will be revealed."

I sat back, dissatisfied. "I understand what you're saying, Swami, but there must be something you can tell me."

"I *am* telling you something very important," he replied. "If you understand the gift I'm giving you, then you will be able to move into this mystery in a way that words can never penetrate or comprehend. You are being guided, just as I said. And yet it isn't your mind where these lessons exist; it's in your soul. Listen to your soul, and it will guide you to where you need to go and whom you should go with. This is a journey you must take . . . it isn't a destination. It is a journey into your own heart, Jimmy. Trust it and it will trust you. Do you understand what I mean by that?"

"I'm not sure. Trust it and it will trust me?"

"Your soul is waiting only for your trust, and then it will guide you in ways that may seem impossible right now. It needs to trust that you will listen, and you need to trust that what it tells you is the truth. This is a time of great discovery, and the more you're able to surrender to that energy, the easier the lessons will be—and the more profound."

The meeting was over, and I didn't know what to think. Of course, I understood what he said. If someone came to me in the same situation, I would have probably done the same. I was being guided—that was clear—but I was hoping for someone to help me sort through everything I was learning to make sure that I wasn't going off track. Without the Swami, I was on my own again and no closer to the truth than I was before.

Unless he was right, of course. If he was, then I wasn't alone at all. If this was just a way for me to listen to and trust the wisdom that was streaming to me from my soul, then I was headed in the right direction. I left the Bahamas with a mixed sense of relief and anxiety. I was on a sacred journey, one that was getting stranger and stranger by the moment. The last thing I wanted was for it to end . . . but of course it didn't.

CHAPTER 2

The Flawed Genius

I decided to e-mail my friend Phil Gruber and ask for some guidance and his thoughts on the matter. Phil has an encyclopedic knowledge of metaphysics, and if he was willing to help me, then I knew I would soon be able to grasp everything I seemed to be missing. After a few days, I received a reply from him: "So, you want to know about the Yud and how it applies to the Moses Code? I'll meet you in Switzerland and explain everything. Maybe we'll even have an adventure or two. . . ."

There was nothing unusual about Phil simply showing up in my life in the strangest of circumstances or when I least expected it. Whether in the Highlands of Scotland or a tiny village in Israel near the Sea of Galilee, he took great delight in surprising me. I'd seen him a couple of months earlier when he came to Madison and Chicago for public screenings of the rough cut of *The Moses Code*. After the Chicago screening, Phil had flown to Singapore, after which he was going to stop off in Bangkok on the way to Melbourne, Australia, to visit his girlfriend. While in Singapore, however, he fell into a very bad depression and needed to return to the States far sooner than planned. He was staying with his sister in Austin, Texas, when he called to tell me what had happened. He wanted to surprise me in Geneva, but given his fragile condition, he wasn't sure if he was up for it. He had been severely depressed when his first marriage fell apart, and over the course of our friendship, I knew that he had suffered occasional bouts of depression. The old saying "To those who much is given, much is required" is certainly true of my friend.

Phil is one of the most brilliant and interesting people I've ever met. He characterizes himself as a "flawed genius," which I've always found a bit strange. He told me that the first time his mother came to see him lecture years earlier, she said, "I didn't understand a word you said, but you looked happy." The scope of his knowledge is beyond remarkable, and when he speaks on esoteric subjects, my mind usually reels. And his rapid-fire brain is so sharp and his speech is so fast that I usually only digest about 30 percent of what he says. Once when I was traveling through Australia, Phil showed up unexpectedly (in his usual style), and I invited him to speak to several groups I was leading. He brought along his Autoharp, an instrument that's deeply soothing, and I noticed that when he sat and just played or played while he was speaking, it helped slow him down. His words were more measured, and he was more fully present. Since then, I've always been happy when he has brought his harp along. When he's on a roll, he's really something to watch. Still, I like it when the calmer, mellower side of him comes out.

The fact that he was waiting for me as I exited Swiss customs was no great surprise. Phil's decision to drop everything and travel on such short notice made me wonder if his information was more urgent than I'd thought it might be. It also made me question whether he'd made the right decision about coming at all. Given his most recent bout with depression, I wondered if it was more important for him to rest at his sister's home than help me. On the other hand, the other reason for his being there could be that my soul had actually called him. As strange as it sounds, at the moment, it felt like the more probable explanation. I smiled when I saw him and then braced myself for the steps to come.

"Jimmy! Over here!" he exclaimed, as he waved his arm back and forth. He was wearing a red beret and oversized jeans. I could also see his luggage sitting next to him, which consisted of just a backpack and a shoulder bag. There was one other bag at his side, the case that held his harp. I was happy to see that he'd brought it. "Over here, Jimmy." I walked in his direction and sat my guitar down to give him a hug.

"I can't believe you're here at the airport," I said to him. "What, no surprises or sudden appearances in the middle of nowhere? I'm almost disappointed."

"Don't be disappointed," he said. "I know it's not my usual thing, but I felt this was too important and had to come. I have so much I need to tell you, and I wouldn't have turned down your invitation for the world. I think you know that. You're really onto something here, and you know how hard it is for me to resist."

The words ran from his mouth almost faster than I could hear them. I knew he was excited, and that was good. At the same time, I didn't want him to get so wound up that he wouldn't get the rest he so badly needed. I looked into his eyes for a sign. They were clear, which was a relief.

"Mr. Twyman? Are you James Twyman?"

I turned around to see five people standing behind me. The woman speaking had dark skin and kind eyes. They all seemed relieved and happy to find me.

"Yes, I am."

"I'm Christiane, the sponsor for your events here in Switzerland," she said to me, reaching out her hand. "Your flight was late . . . we were beginning to worry."

"Yes, I'm afraid it was," I said. I shook her hand and then said hello to the others who were with her.

"These are my friends who wanted to help escort you," she said.

"And this is my friend, Phil Gruber. I don't remember if I told you that he was coming."

"No problem," said the man standing next to Christiane. "We brought three cars, so there's plenty of room."

I nodded at Phil. He looked relaxed, but I sensed he was still fragile beneath a brave veneer. Moments later, we were loading our luggage into a small van and exiting the airport.

"There's so much I want to tell you," Phil told me as we climbed into the backseat. "More than you might imagine."

"I had that feeling. You're being more mysterious than I expected, though."

He was quiet for a moment as if he was wondering what, or how much, he should say.

"When I say 'more than you might imagine,'" he continued, "what I mean is that we have work to do. We have an awesome opportunity here. Of course, it has to do with the Yud, but that's only the tip of the iceberg."

"Now you're really being mysterious," I said.

"If I tell you everything now, you might want to send me back," he quipped, smiling, although I knew he was being serious. "I'm not trying to freak you out or anything . . . well, maybe just a little. This is some pretty serious stuff, and it has to be entered into with trust, dedication, determination, awareness, and conviction."

I sat up in my seat and must have raised my voice a bit because our new friends in the front turned around slightly to see what was going on. Luckily, their English wasn't fluent enough to understand.

"What are you talking about? I thought you were going to tell me why the Moses Code was really a Yud. I was hoping that you'd fill in the missing spaces."

"This is way beyond what you're calling the Moses Code," Phil remarked. "I think it's more than you can wrap your head around right now. There are forces at work here that you don't understand."

"I took notes based on our phone conversations and the e-mails you sent," I replied, taking out my pad. "You said that we're dealing with ancient mysteries so powerful that there are those who would like to protect them. Actually, you wrote that these so-called protectors aren't necessarily people, but something more elusive. You also said something about angels protecting certain mysteries because of sacred seals or pacts between them and God, as well as something about demons being somehow locked into patterns they can't escape . . . or don't want to. Is that right? These beings are imprisoned in multidimensional fields that lock them in place, and in some cases, they don't even know they've been captured. Am I getting this right? You also said that it's time for them to be released—that it's time for the pacts the angels made with God to finally be fulfilled."

"More or less," Phil replied, obviously delighted by the fact that I was serious enough to actually take notes.

"But Phil, what does this have to do with the Yud? I had no idea we were stepping into a Dan Brown novel."

"This is more than a novel," he said, his tone becoming more serious. "This is real, and it's important. I also don't think I'm exaggerating when I say that so much depends on it."

I took a deep breath and sat back in my seat. Things had suddenly taken a dramatic and unexpected turn.

✡✡✡

I first met Phil at a spiritual conference in Colorado in 1996. I saw him in the cafeteria the Monday after the conference ended and remember seeing a double rainbow out the window. I was heading back to my table carrying a full tray of food when, seemingly out of nowhere, Phil appeared in front of me, blocking my way. At first I was a little taken aback, but there was something about his eyes—something that attracted me on a very deep level. They danced around like the flame of a bright candle, and behind them was an energy that he couldn't seem to contain.

He immediately launched into a five-minute dissertation on the meaning and metaphysical implications of my name. I couldn't repeat it if I tried. The very next day, I was in downtown Boulder with my daughter, Angela. My van had broken down, and I was killing time in a metaphysical bookstore when I ran into Phil again. It was like no time had passed, and he immediately continued his discourse on my name from where he left off. I knew it wouldn't be the last I'd see of him.

"Tell me what you know about the Yud," I said to Phil when we were settled in our hotel in downtown Lausanne. We sat at a small table in the lobby and tried to maintain a healthy distance from the other guests. "You were there at the test screenings of *The Moses Code* in Madison and Chicago, and you told me that you saw the final version in Austin."

"The Yud and the Moses Code are just the beginning," he replied. "From the moment the comma flashed on the screen, I knew you were onto something—it's the tip of the iceberg, as I said before. You must know or at least suspect that there's a whole lot more beneath the surface."

"I didn't know that at first," I confessed, taking a sip of water. "I honestly thought that it really was a comma. I'm not Jewish, and I had no idea what a Yud was. Since then, though, it's all I've been hearing about."

"I'm not surprised. Let me tell you a few things about the Yud, and then you'll know how close you are. The Yud is the tenth and smallest letter of the Hebrew alphabet. Each letter of this specialized alphabet is a crystallization of an aspect of the Divine Word, or the Sacred Name. The Yud is the building block from which all other letters are generated. It has been said that all the other letters are generated by its movement."

Phil took out a notepad and drew a Yud for me. It reminded me of a flame, or a flag unfurling in a breeze. It also reminded me of a comma.

"This is getting interesting," I said. "Keep going."

"For many, the Yud is *being,* pure being—a symbol of the omnipresence of God in the world. It's also the smallest letter and represents the primal vibration of the Universe. It's the only Hebrew letter literally suspended in space—a bridge between worlds, you might say. The beautiful thing is that within the Yud is held the potential of all things to come into manifest being. It may very well be the point of light in the mind and heart of God . . . a point of condensed love and light, or what some people call the 'middle point.' It teaches us that within the smallest of things lies the greatest potential for creation."

"I also heard that the Yud represents the hand of God," I said. "But the real question is, 'What does that mean?' Is it a real hand or a metaphorical one? Or both? If God had a hand, what would it look like? Would it sweep through the sky like some kind of Michelangelesque nightmare, or would it be like a gentle wind?"

"The hand of God is definitely reaching down from Heaven right now," Phil said, "but it may not be as gentle as we would like to think. There was a time when it could have been, but no longer. There are no simple answers, and the clock is ticking."

"What would you say it is?" I asked, sensing the urgency that was beginning to show in his voice.

"I'd say that the Yud is like a pause that's pregnant with possibility. The use of the comma in *The Moses Code* was a brilliant stroke. It creates the pause that allows Divine Inspiration to enter. Commas also connect; they are bridges. But the pause, to me, is the key. Are you familiar with *The Essene Gospel of Peace* and the third communion with the Angel of Air?

"*The Essene Gospel of Peace* . . . yes. Wasn't that the one translated by Edmond Bordeaux Szekely?"

"Szekely had access to the secret vaults within the Vatican," Phil said. "The gospel he found talks about the 'Holy Breath which is placed higher than all the other things created.' It says that between the breathing in and the breathing out is contained all the mysteries of the Infinite Garden. The comma allows for that pause."

"That's an interesting parallel," I remarked. "Is there anything else you can tell me about the Yud?"

"Like I said, the Yud is the smallest letter in the Hebrew alphabet and is commonly understood to represent the finger of God that points the way. It can also symbolize the hand—the hand being a symbol of the power of creative or directed energy. You see, the closed hand, or fist, signifies Unity, the Creator. The open fist is the symbol of man and our inborn potential to re-evolve back into Oneness. In fact, the Hebrew word for hand is *yad*. It's the middle point. Also, the yin-yang symbol is a representation of two Yuds in the harmonious flow of dynamic equilibrium. The Yud, like all the others, is a letter of fire, or of flame—meaning that the letters of the alphabet are expressions of the Creative Fire out of which all things are born and into which all things will eventually return. It connects one to that Great Creative Fire. Each letter is an aspect of that Creative Force."

"That's why Moses's burning bush wasn't consumed by the flames," I offered. "This is what I wanted to bring out in *The Moses Code:* the information that Moses needed was already within him, just as it is already within us. Fire gets the energy moving, like electrons that begin firing and revealing their hidden qualities. That's what needs to happen to each one of us. We need to burn inside a bit."

"A Divine Burn."

"Right . . . exactly. We burn and become like popcorn kernels that suddenly explode into something new."

"I'm never going to look at popcorn the same way again," Phil said, laughing. "But seriously, time, as we perceive it with our linear minds, is speeding up, accelerating. There's not a moment to waste. When I saw the movie, I knew you were ready."

"What am I ready for?"

"You're ready to do a lot more than talk about the Moses Code," Phil answered. "You're also ready to do more than write about how the Divine Name was revealed to Moses and how to use the secrets contained within it. It was a step, I'll grant you, a rather large step, but you're ready to do something much more important—and much more dangerous."

"Why dangerous? I'm not one to shy away from danger, but I have to know if this is real or just some kind of lesson you're trying to teach me. You spoke on the phone about demons and angels guarding ancient seals or being caught in some elaborate trap. How much of that is true?"

"Whatever you're willing to allow yourself to believe is true. What do you think?"

"I think I really need to understand the meaning of Kabbalah before I go any further," I said. "Everything I learn keeps coming back to it, but since I have no background, I can't see how everything fits together."

"Okay, let me give you a quick introduction into the ancient mystical teachings of the Jewish people: the Kabbalah, or *ha-Kabbalah*, is a uniquely Jewish construction." He sat back in his chair for dramatic effect. "The earliest writings that scholars usually associate with it date from around 2,000 years ago, although much of the source material for what we understand today as Kabbalah has its origins in remote antiquity. Ancient texts talk about what were called *Merkabah mystics*. The ultimate goal of these *Merkubalim*, as they were known, was the penetration into the seven Halls of Creation in order to reach a place called Merkabah, the throne chariot of God."

"What's the throne chariot of God?" I asked him.

"It's a vehicle that can be used to ascend to the Higher Heavenly Realms—to literally penetrate the magnetic veils that normally separate us from a fuller experience of God. The *Merkabah Vehicle, Jeweled Vehicle,* or *Sweet Chariot* as it's sometimes known, can take you all the way to the throne of God, to stand before the face of the Ancient of Days, as expressed in some traditions. The Sefer Yetzirah, the Book of Formation, is considered by many to be the first text of Jewish occult mysticism, and it's attributed to Abraham. It discusses, among other things, the manipulation of sacred letters in the construction of the world.

"What we normally understand to be Kabbalah, in a more modern sense, dates to 12th-century Provence to a book called the Sefer ha-Bahir, the Book of Brilliant Light. Later, the Sefer ha-Zohar (the Book of Splendor, or Radiance), dating from 13th-century Spain, was a revelation to the great Kabbalist Moses De León, after which he later organized and collated this vast body of occult mystical knowledge. De León claimed that it contained the mystical writings of Shimon bar Yohai, a rabbi who lived in the 2nd century. Evidence suggests that the origin of the material compiled by De León, which has come to be known as the Zohar, goes even further back in history. But there are some serious things to consider before we embark on this journey . . . before we enter the *Chapel Perilous*."

"And that's why you keep telling me that this is a dangerous journey," I said, almost laughingly.

"*Challenging* is a better word, actually; and if we're going to do this together, you're going to need to take it much more seriously." He looked more composed and seemed to have a sense of purpose I hadn't noticed before. "This isn't some kind of New Age fantasy. It's a real, mystical journey that requires extreme discipline, diligence, and preparation; and that's just for starters. What we're going to attempt to do, to my knowledge, has never been attempted before, at least successfully. And if we're successful, it will change much in the world, hopefully for the better. If we're not, then we take the risk of being torn apart like the Christians in the Colosseum. And to tell you the truth, the planet as a whole might not fare any better. I wish I was joking, but I'm not."

"Okay, let's keep going before you really scare me. Tell me more about the Kabbalah."

"Fine. The origin of the word *Kabbalah* is attributed to a man named Isaac the Blind who lived in the 12th and 13th centuries. It's usually defined as 'to receive' or 'to accept,' also 'that which has been handed down,' as well as 'tradition.' There are more esoteric meanings, but these are the ones most commonly associated with it. I'll give you a little clue, though. They all have to do with the relationship of the words *KA, BA,* and *LAH.* The uniquely Jewish esoteric or mystical tradition known as Kabbalah is rumored to be the world's oldest body of spiritual knowledge. Within the body of Kabbalistic writings is encoded ancient secrets, long-hidden keys to the creation and structure of the Universe, and how that design structure is mirrored in ourselves. Kabbalah penetrates to the deeper mysteries of the human heart and soul . . . of the material and nonmaterial realms. It explores the physical and metaphysical nature of humanity, as well as our origins and evolutionary destinies—those kinds of things.

"The true origins of Kabbalah are shrouded in mystery and speculation, lost in the mists of time. It is said that, along with the written Torah that was given to Moses at Mount Sinai, he also received an oral tradition, which in all respects explains the vast secrets and mysteries encoded in the Torah. Before Moses, the direct transmission of the true nature of the Law, as given by Yahweh, was offered sparingly to select individuals to provide a road map to a very special place . . . a preexistent Heaven called the Pleroma—to others, Paradise."

"I spoke with a Swami in the Bahamas," I told Phil, "who is also a Kabbalah expert, and he said that the true Kabbalah is not the one that is written but the one that is revealed through direct revelation."

"That's correct. Gnosis, or direct revelation, is the name of the game, and that's what Moses received. It's said that he received the Law during the day, but the explanation of the Law during the night. But he wasn't the only one. Some Kabbalists say that there have been five direct transmissions of the inner teaching, and a few believe that there will be at least one more.

"The first is said to have been given to a band of fallen angels. The second was given to Adam by the fallen angel Raziel, the Keeper of Secrets, as a road map back to Paradise, although the angel Uriel and God's Good Angels would beg to differ. There was an original innocence we enjoyed before the fall into the illusion of separation, where we fully understood the secret of creation. It was at this point in our evolution that we were given the Kabbalah. That's what I mean when I say it was given to Adam, not necessarily a man of flesh and blood, but more a representation of our original innocence. Anyway, the third transmission was given to Abraham, the father of the three great monotheistic religions—Judaism, Christianity, and Islam—and through Abraham to his three sons. The fourth was Noah, who, with his floating zoo, alighted on the top of Mount Ararat in Turkey. The fifth was Moses."

"Do you think it ends there?" I asked.

"No, I don't, but that would be getting ahead of ourselves. The point I'm trying to make is that the true Torah was more than what was written down. There is an esoteric wisdom and eternal mystery that has been encoded into the written law that didn't end up on Moses's Tablets of Testimony."

"Would it be fair to say that Jesus was another to receive the full transmission of the teaching?"

"Now that's tricky, Jimmy. Certainly Jesus, from his travels and having sat at the feet of many masters, and as an Essene initiate, as well as an adept in Egyptian and Hebraic Secret Sciences, would have in all probability been familiar with a great many esoteric doctrines. I'm sure he was well versed in not only the secrets of creation and re-creation, but the origin and destiny of all souls. In other words, the answer would be *yes*."

"Is it possible that Jesus had the fullest comprehension of all his predecessors?" I asked.

"Who can say? Most Jews, of course, don't recognize Jesus's legitimacy—certainly not as the 'expected one,' the Messiah. It's argued that he never claimed that for himself. When he said, 'I have not come to claim the Torah, only to fulfill it,' the door was opened for a lot of possible interpretations. When Jesus was in the Temple, he said, 'Before Abraham was, I AM.'"

"He was claiming that he was one with God," I noted.

"Yes. I AM is how God is known to himself. I believe that Jesus understood God's revelation, and you can bet that didn't sit well with the priestly elite of the time. Speaking of the priestly elite, you also need to understand something. At certain points in the tradition, there were extremely strict laws determining who could even study the Kabbalah. In early Kabbalistic traditions, and even now, transmission came directly from a master, or a teacher, to his chosen pupils or disciples. Even today, in more Orthodox circles, if you're a woman, you can forget about it, although there are records of women back in the day who, contrary to popular opinion, were well versed in many of the deeper mysteries of consciousness. One such woman was Noa, one of the daughters of Zelophehad. There was also Sarah, Miriam, Esther, Devorah, and many others, not to mention the Magdalene.

"Even nowadays, to be considered a serious student of Kabbalah in certain circles, you must be male, 40 years of age or older, married, have at least three children, and most important, you must be Jewish. All that's changing now, but prior to the 17th century, there were no such restrictions, so when modern Kabbalists try to impose these rules, they really don't have much, if any, historical precedent—not to mention a leg to stand on."

"It's almost like most Catholics believing that it has always been a rule that priests remain celibate and can't marry," I said. "It's actually only been a strict rule for about half the life of the church, about a thousand years."

"That's correct," Phil confirmed, "but let's stay on the subject so I don't forget where I am. This may seem like an endless amount of information that may or may not have any relevance for you, but it's significant, as you'll no doubt find out for yourself. The final thing I want to tell you regarding the historic transmissions of the Kabbalah is perhaps the most crucial. This is not a common belief among all teachers of the tradition but was and still is believed by some, perhaps more than one would think. As I've mentioned, most believe that God has revealed the true and full Kabbalah five times, possibly six, but there is rumored to be a final time that is still left to come. This will be the most important transmission, and it will determine the fate of this planet."

"Do you know whom it will be given to?"

"Yes, I believe I do."

There was a long pause. I could feel goose bumps forming on the surface of my entire body. "Okay," I said, "can you tell me?"

Another long moment of silence. Finally, Phil looked at me. "It will be given to *you*."

"Me?" I asked, swallowing hard. "Why me? What are you saying?"

He leaned forward and said, "Let me be very clear. I mean you and me and everyone. The final transmission is for all of us . . . for humanity itself. The stage has been set for the ultimate revelation that will change everything on the planet. There's an evolutionary leap that is about to take place that has, in fact, already begun. Whether it comes peacefully, with ease and grace like that gentle breeze you were talking about earlier, I'm not sure. All I know is that it's inevitable. A table has been set and an invitation has gone out. What was formerly reserved for the privileged few, such as

Moses and Jesus, is being offered to all. Our continued presence on Earth is at stake, and as always, God has heard our prayers."

Phil closed his eyes and leaned back in his chair. A waiter walked into the lobby at that moment and asked if we wanted anything. I took a deep breath, welcomed the momentary break, and ordered a cappuccino. Phil didn't look like he needed one.

"You know, Phil, this isn't terribly different from what many people say about the Second Coming of Christ—meaning that it won't be a single person, like the physical return of Jesus, but that the consciousness of Christ would open for all of us, and each one of us will be able to embrace the same light and energy that Jesus enjoyed 2,000 years ago. Do you think there's a correlation?"

"We're really saying the same thing," he replied. "This is ultimately about embracing and embodying the teachings of freedom and truth, the inner esoteric as well as the common, or outer exoteric. This is about a second birth—the birth of something holy in each and every one of us. Jesus said that when he addressed huge crowds, he had to tell them stories, parables about God. They weren't able to understand him in any other way. Jesus also realized that most of his closest disciples didn't have the foggiest notion what he was trying to express. Look it up. It would seem that only Mary Magdalene and maybe a few others had any clue at all.

"The time has come where we all need to be ready to receive the revelation of the secret teachings of the ages, and believe me, it's required now more than ever. What's currently happening on the planet is completely unprecedented, as far as I know. We stand on the brink of destroying our entire world or of re-creating another one altogether. Everything we've done over countless lifetimes has bought us to this point, and if we would only realize certain truths and practice them day to day in a practical way, then we would turn again toward peace. It's time for us to finally understand the true nature of God, our indelible connection and relationship to the Source of *All That Is*, and the greater meaning and purpose of our lives. That is what the Kabbalah and all works of higher calling are all about."

I took a big gulp of air, trying to absorb everything Phil was telling me.

"Let me get back to the Torah for a moment," he continued. "There is the Revealed Torah, or Law, called the Pentateuch, which consists of the first five books of Moses. But then there's a hidden, secret Torah called Sod, which describes the nature of God, the origins and destiny of the cosmos, and the nature of man. All observant Jews believe, at least they are presumed to believe, that the Torah is the Word of God and that Hebrew is the Language of Creation. The Kabbalah, on the other hand, is said to be the initiated understanding of the Torah and of all the Divine powers of creation; and when working with the Kabbalah, one can literally unlock its secrets and share in the boundless joy that is our birthright. The Torah is the template or blueprint of creation. It reveals the Laws of Creation and even God's secret, not to mention how to live in the highest way day to day.

"But without the initiated understanding of Kabbalah, we can't read the blueprint. It remains a mystery until the inner teaching is revealed, experienced, actually lived every day—and that's the invitation, and the challenge, we're being given now. And remember, even Kabbalah has its exoteric and esoteric faces."

"It's all very exciting," I said, "but it's also a little scary. It sounds like you're saying that we have to learn this . . . or else."

"That is what I'm saying. The question then becomes 'What is the *what else*?' What will happen if we don't? All I know is that if *soft* love doesn't work, then *tough* love might be required. The earth is always renewing itself, and if we can't learn these lessons, then it will renew us, although not gently. We see it happening all around us already. Actions taken and not taken are threatening our very survival, not to mention the very real possibility of someone possessed pushing the button and bringing about our complete annihilation. If we don't wake up and begin to live by Divine Right Law, we'll all be up the pond without a paddle, so to speak."

"What can we do about it?" I asked. "I hope you're not going to go completely doom and gloom on me and not offer any kind of solution."

"Not at all," Phil assured me. "I'm not a doom and gloomer. Listen, you're the one who unlocked the Moses Code, and now it's time to unlock another code. You were only scratching the surface in what you did before. You were right in everything you said and wrote, all about the name of God unlocking the experience of our oneness and ability to create miracles. But that was just one name. The *Ehyeh Asher Ehyeh,* or I AM THAT I AM, is one, but there are nine more names, all of which point to different aspects of the Divine. You need to unlock the secrets encoded in those as well, and when you do, more mysteries will be revealed and more loving grace can flow in and through this world."

"These names you're talking about . . . do they form some kind of code?" I asked.

"Absolutely. It's why fate brought us together again. There are multiple levels of coding in all works of higher calling, including the Kabbalah. And there's one set of codes that I believe we're meant to use in some very special places."

"And I'm sure that somehow brings us back to the angels and demons," I said. "Everything seems to lead there."

"All I can tell you right now is that where we're going, there are many of both that are imprisoned and aren't able to break free. They're imprisoned by forces we can't completely understand, but the proper use of the Sacred Names can help set them free, and in the process, it can also liberate us. When we're free, very specialized channels of energy will be able to flow again. There's one spot on this planet where this is most true, and that's where we're going next."

"Can you tell me where that is?" I asked.

"Of course I can. We're going to Paris."

✿✿✿✿✿

CHAPTER 3

A Kabbalist in Paris

Three days later when the conference was over in Switzerland, we were on the TGV, the fast train to Paris, and I had the familiar sensation that my life was about to change. Phil sat opposite me and didn't seem interested in talking. This, of course, only made me want to talk more. The countryside rushed by at dizzying speeds, and an occasional farmhouse broke the monotony . . . then it, too, was gone in a split second. Was it a symbol of my own life—the fast pace I'd been living and the speed in which one chapter would end and another would begin? I was glad Phil was with me to mark this new beginning, but the mysteriousness of this adventure made me wonder if I was ready to step forward onto this ancient and mystical path—a road I knew little, if anything, about . . . the path of Kabbalah. I was less than a novice, but that didn't seem to slow me down or dampen my enthusiasm.

"I can't stop thinking about everything you've told me so far," I said to Phil as the conductor came to check our tickets. "I feel like I'm only scratching the surface, and it's so rich and profound. It makes me want to learn everything I can."

"You can study Kabbalah for a lifetime . . . lifetimes, in fact, and only scratch the surface," he replied, wiping his eyes as if waking up from a dream. Neither of us had slept much during our time in Switzerland. Paris was consuming our thoughts, and yet the adventure felt as if it would never really arrive. "It's like a well that has no bottom. You throw a rock in and wait for the sound of splashing water, but it never comes. That's because it's fathomless, like God. According to traditional Kabbalah, we can't fully understand the infinity of God since the true essence of God is unknowable, unattainable. At the same time, it's said that Kabbalah goes into the very essence of God; encoded in its very matrix are templates—literal maps and keys that are essential in understanding the mysteries of cosmic creation. Your swami friend told you that the true Kabbalah can't be written down, that it can only be experienced. Well, yes *and* no. I would agree with him insofar as when you write something down, a piece is lost because you've attempted to translate the infinite into the finite. But if you can remain open enough to simply allow it to flow into you, then you actually become its essence. And that's the real goal, isn't it?"

"I think at one point you told me that from the perspective of Jewish thought, thinking of oneself as being one with or an embodiment of God is blasphemy."

"Absolutely!" Phil exclaimed. "The furthest a mystic Jew is willing to venture is to say that he's been able to contemplate the Divine Majesty. To say 'I am God' or 'I am one with God' is a big no-no. No form of nonheretical Jewish thought would speak of even the possibility of a human being becoming Divine in this world, for it's impossible to have unity with the Divine while on Earth. To do so would be heresy."

"Okay," I said. "So that's what Jewish mystics believe. How about you? What do you say?"

Phil looked at me and grinned. "What would you guess I believe?"

I put down the book I'd been reading. "I think we believe the same: the purpose of life is to realize that we are one with God, pure and simple. I believe that the single goal of our soul's purpose here on Earth is to remember the truth of our Divine Nature."

"Yes, in essence I would agree. The goal is to access the infinite within, to reconcile our dual natures, to achieve the state known as

Devekut: spiritual Divine Union, the union of man and his Creator, resulting in a reunification with God that changes everything."

"A reunification with God?"

"Sure. If I say that you're re-merging with God, then it wouldn't be entirely accurate." Phil continued, "You can't re-merge with something or someone that you've never been truly separated from. However, you can emerge from your sleeping state, your belief in separation, or the illusion of separation, and realize what has always been true—that you are one with God. That's the power of the Moses Code: it stimulates a remembering of the union that everything is contained within you, and you are contained within everything.

"The name God gave to Moses, *Ehyeh Asher Ehyeh,* or simply *Ehyeh,* meaning I AM, was meant to describe God's revelation of his personal *beingness.* It was meant to show Moses, and us, that God is everywhere and in everything—that everything exists within a unified field of dimensionalized consciousness. And when you chant the name, as you wrote in *The Moses Code,* you begin sensing that oneness within yourself because, of course, you are one with God and you can identify with the power of God within yourself, just as Moses did. You can't sense the Universal oneness of God without also realizing it within yourself."

"Which seems to be where most religions go off the mark," I added. "Teaching people that they have a direct line to God makes it pretty difficult to control them or make them do what they want."

"And why do you think they want that?"

"For people to follow the rules?"

"Yes. Why?"

"Because every religion, in the end, wants to survive and grow, and the only way it can do that is by establishing a set of rules or dogmas that everyone must follow. People love that. They love to be told what to do or believe because it removes personal revelation from the equation—"

"Not to mention personal responsibility."

"You bet," I said. "And yet it can never really be removed

33

because every spiritual tradition has its mystics, and they all pretty much seek the same thing: union with God."

"So would you say that the experience of oneness is the goal of every mystic?" Phil asked.

"I think so, yes. A Christian mystic seeks union with the consciousness of Christ, a Buddhist with the Buddha nature, and a Hindu with Brahman."

"Are you saying that the organized religions themselves don't encourage this? Do you think they want people to remain separate from each other, from God, and to exclude everyone who doesn't agree with their view of things?"

"Take a baptized Christian, for example," I said, leaning in closer. "Either you form a part of the body of Christ or else. . . ."

"Or else it's the highway, right?"

"I don't want to make any absolute statements about all religions," I quickly added, as I was starting to feel a bit uncomfortable with my directness. "But in general that's probably true."

"So does that mean that we should avoid religions and simply seek our own mystical experiences?" Phil asked, obviously noticing my discomfort. It felt as if he was leading me in a particular direction, but I was unclear where it was. I was trying to be careful not to step into a trap, but then I decided to relax and simply say whatever came to me.

"I'll tell you what I believe," I said. "The answer is no. I don't think people should avoid honoring or practicing a particular religion if that's what they're drawn to. There's definitely value, especially in following well-laid spiritual paths that have been working for thousands of years. I think this is one of the biggest problems in many New Age circles—that anything goes no matter how far-out or weird. People will buy anything these days. Do you believe that I was at an event last year where a woman actually claimed to be channeling her cat whom she believes to be an ascended master? And people were lining up to hear what the cat had to say. That's the kind of thing that drives me crazy: people throwing away their common sense. I think that there needs to be a balance. We need to look to the traditions of our various religions and learn from them but also be open to the particular ways that Spirit is revealing itself in our lives."

"Think about it," Phil remarked. "Kabbalah is an initiated understanding of the Torah. Remember me telling you that according to the teachings, the Torah is considered the Word of God and was formulated before the creation of the world? An old teacher of mine said that Kabbalah doesn't just tread water on the surface, so to speak. It dives deep into the mysteries that fill every sentence of every page, and, in so doing, helps people access their own connection with the Divine, furthering a closer, personal relationship with God. The Torah is literally a template or blueprint of creation, and the Kabbalah aims to define its inner meaning and structure. It's nothing less than God's revelation to its creation."

"Would you say that the name of God that was given to Moses at the burning bush was at the very heart of what became the three monotheistic religions, beginning, of course, with Abraham?" I inquired.

"I would venture to say that the name given to Moses at the burning bush . . . or more precisely, the meaning of the name given to Moses that fateful day is what lies at the heart of all systems of religious and spiritual thought. Before Moses, even before Abraham, the seeds of what would become the Judeo-Christian tradition were already present. But when Moses had his experience at Mount Sinai, everything changed—not only for those of the Hebrew persuasion, but by extension, the ebb and flow of history."

"So you would agree that the name has important implications in our modern world?"

"I would." Phil continued, "Today we have an altogether different mind-set and a somewhat different take on history, not just biblical antecedents. But looking at it historically, Moses came and asked God one of the most important questions in history: 'What is your name?' Until then, the children of Israel didn't identify the power of the Almighty with their own, keeping the Divine at arm's length, you might say.

"Suddenly, God got up close and personal, and the revelation of his Most Holy Name on Mount Sinai that fateful day was born of a desire to enter into a special covenant with his chosen people. God and his chosen people were on a first-name basis. Moses could now identify the power of God with his own, one of the most powerful lessons in *The Moses Code*. God was something he could apprehend, although still not completely. But through the power of the name, he could use it to manifest miracles in his life and in the lives of the people he was entrusted to lead to freedom."

"Like the plagues?"

"They were terrible miracles, to be sure. But they proved something. It proved that there was great power in being conscious of an eternal, intrinsic connection to the source of Divinity within; the indwelling presence of God; and a reappraisal of the concept of *shi'ur komma,* the 'measure of man' in relation to God—in other words, how we measure up."

"The word *komma* sure sounds a lot like *comma,*" I offered, suddenly getting the connection between his words and what I've written and lectured about on the Moses Code.

"That ain't the half of it. It proved that the power of God, revealed in the name, was within them all the time—later to be understood as 'the kingdom of Heaven,' a source of power and personal revelation and a portal into what's called the Vault of the Adepts, the source of all true magic and miracles."

"That was the name I AM THAT I AM."

"Well, this is where it gets interesting," Phil said. "*Ehyeh Asher Ehyeh* was only one name given to Moses, by way of an introduction. Immediately after God said *Ehyeh Asher Ehyeh,* which in standard Masoretic texts is translated as I AM THAT I AM, God said, 'Say this to the people of Israel: I AM has sent me to you.' Now this is the true name of God, at least from this perspective of the Angel of the Lord, whom God chose to speak through."

"The Angel of the Lord?"

"Yes, the same angel who told Jacob that the secret of the name would not be revealed until the time of the Second Coming, or the Second Adam, according to an interpretation by Rudolf Steiner, the founder of the Waldorf education system. You see, *Ehyeh Asher Ehyeh* has a multiplicity of meanings. A favorite of mine is: 'I am in the process of *becoming* what I will myself to be' or 'I will be what I will be.' You see, Jimmy, it's about choice—that is, the exercise of free will."

"Is it the same as saying Yahweh?" I asked.

"Now that's a horse of a different color. Yahweh is a common spelling for what is known as the Tetragrammaton, the second name given to Moses, which in English is 'I AM.' The word comes from the Greek: *tetra* meaning 'four' and *gramma* meaning 'letter.' It signifies the four letters that have the power to harness the most powerful forces in creation simply by correctly pronouncing this Divine Name. Those four letters are 'Yud Heh Vav Heh,' and we refer to it as *Shem ha-Meforesh,* meaning 'the name of distinction or excellence.' This name is the source of all the sacred names, and within its very structure the blueprint of all creation is found. Even the contemplation of this name can unleash forces virtually beyond comprehension, at least in relation to our limited human minds.

"And as you know," he continued, "it's never supposed to be pronounced, not even written, for once God's name is written, it can be erased, altered, or discarded. That's why the words *Adonai* or *Elohim* are substituted for the Tetragrammaton. This is out of respect for the Ineffable Name. Taking the name of God in vain is forbidden, as stated in the third of the Ten Commandments. There was also the ever-present threat of being branded as a blasphemer, yet it has been argued that at the time of the Torah and the prophets, no such prohibition was in effect."

"So how did that rule come about?"

"Listen, Jimmy, I'm all for respecting the force that such a powerful name can unleash," he declared with words that seemed to bite hard.

"Yes, but sometimes respect can lead one to throw away the very gifts that could transform the world," I countered.

"Right. That's like throwing away the baby with the bathwater. There are many references in the Old Testament, Genesis, Joel, and in many of the Psalms, for example, where the name of Yahweh was celebrated and exalted. Look at Isaiah 12:4: 'Give thanks to YHWH.

37

Call his name aloud.' There are references found in the Talmud and the Mishna prohibiting the pronunciation of the name, although this is a matter of heated debate in Talmudic circles. As things turned out, with the exception of certain prayerful states or acts of benediction, only the High Priest, the Kohen Gadol, after a series of purifications, would recite the name ten times and only during Yom Kippur."

"What is it in a name that gives it so much power?"

"You sound like Alice when you ask that. When Alice asked Humpty Dumpty why a name is so important, he replied: 'My name means the shape *I am.*' Are you starting to get it?"

Phil started to get that faraway look in his eyes. I'd seen it before, especially when he'd begin lacing his explanations with colorful metaphors drawn from books like *Alice in Wonderland* or *The Lord of the Rings*. I noticed his eyes begin to focus again, and thankfully, he continued. "In Kabbalah, it is written that 'I AM my Name,' which suggests that the power of God is in his very name. And by *very*, I mean *true*—God's true name: I AM, the Tetragrammaton. In the Hindu Advaita Vedanta, the I AM is what's known as an abstraction in the mind of the stateless state, the absolute, supreme reality."

"Parabrahman."

"Exactly . . . pure awareness. In the Mahavakyas, the four great sayings in Advaita, the I AM THAT is echoed in the *Tat Tvam Asi,* 'Thou art that' or 'You are that.' It's one of the grand pronouncements of Vedantic Hinduism, and the parallels don't end there. The word *that* comes from the Sanskrit *tat,* meaning 'boundless.' We are boundless, only bounded by our limited beliefs."

"Yes, I know. And Jesus said, 'Whatsoever you ask in my Name, that I will do.' He even went so far as to identify himself as the I AM in the Gospel of John. He understood the power in a name and was able to harness it to create miracles. He was almost stoned to death many times because he said I AM. In doing so, Jesus was claiming the power in God's name and that he was one with God, which is, of course, the source of all knowledge and wisdom, not to mention the ability to produce miracles."

"Now, I want you to look at the letters in the Tetragrammaton." Phil continued, "In Hebrew, the letters read as 'Yud Heh Vav Heh.' Is there anything there that jumps out at you?"

I looked at the letters but nothing sparked my attention. "What am I missing?"

"Of those four letters, there's one that is said to hold the greatest potential for creation, something we've been talking about from the beginning."

I looked again and saw it immediately. "Yes, of course—it's a Yud. The first letter is the Yud, the comma."

"Yes, your comma of the Moses Code. It's the first letter of the Tetragrammaton, the unspeakable personal name of God, considered by many to be the highest name of God, and, as I've mentioned, the only proper name according to the great Kabbalist and philosopher Moses Maimonides. Look at Isaiah again, 42:8: 'I am YHWH, this is my name,' or Exodus 6:3, where God says that he appeared to Abraham, Isaac, and Jacob as El Shaddai, which means 'God Almighty,' but he was not known to them by his name Yahweh. This might be because it's the name God used to seal his covenant with Israel, made after the time of the Patriarchs.

"At any rate, the Tetragrammaton is said to contain the original vibration behind all manifest existence, and the Yud is the primal vibration of creation. The Yud is the gateway to the Creative Fire— out of which all things are born and to which all things inevitably return, a skeleton key that unlocks many of the mysteries of creation and perhaps even the secrets of God. But there are other, many other names that possess enormous power and great importance, and that's where this journey is going to take us now."

"I always thought that the Most Holy Name of God in Hebrew was *Ehyeh Asher Ehyeh,* or simply *Ehyeh,* the name that was given to Moses at the bush," I said, a bit confused.

"Yes, that's correct."

"But God has other names as well . . . like the Tetragrammaton?"

"That's also correct," Phil affirmed. He smiled and had the look of one beginning to unwind a long riddle. "Many other names. Remember that the true essence of God is transcendent, unknowable—it cannot be described. Think of it this way: you have more than one name, or more than one way of calling yourself, depending on the level of intimacy that's called for or what quality you want to bring forth. For example, if I call you Jimmy it has a very different vibration than if I call you James. When you do something publicly, like signing a book, for example, you always sign it as James, but most of your friends call you Jimmy. Do you see how these two names can change the way you act or respond, as well as how people react and respond to you?"

"When you put it that way—"

"That's one of the wonderful things about the many names of God," he added without pausing. "Each name represents a different aspect of not only God, but of each one of us. In a way, the names are a *revealed aspect* of God, and through them, the unfolding knowledge of God's presence is revealed through us as we come to know more of God and express The Presence through their use. God makes itself known to us through these translations of Divine emanations from the limitless light of the *En Sof,* which means 'boundlessness.'"

"I'm not sure I know what you mean, Phil. I know that in this world we like to find ways of identifying ourselves in relationship to others. I've always thought that it's really the ego that does that."

"Think of it this way," he said. "If we're one with God or an embodiment of God—or however you want to express that thought—then there's nothing we can say about the Divine that isn't also true about us. The myriad names of God tell us who we are. They reveal aspects of our truth that have been hidden or disguised by the limited confines of our egotistic mind."

"Can you be a bit more specific on what you mean by *ego?* It's a word we throw around so much, but I'm not sure many people really understand it."

"In Kabbalistic thought, the ego is defined as the will to receive pleasure, but it's for oneself and not to be shared. That's the key. It's a costume our soul wears—a garment that veils or conceals our Divinely inspired natures. Those veils are likened to curtains that block out the Light of God."

"I've always loved the acronym for ego: Edging God Out," I offered. "It's pretty accurate. The ego is the part of us that wants to be alone and isolated, somehow thinking that it makes us stronger. Obviously, that can't be true, but the ego doesn't bother with truth. Its logic is always topsy-turvy. It believes that accepting the truth requires a sacrifice in order to *be* everything. However, nothing needs to be given up to be everything; it's just the idea of giving everything up. Does that make sense?"

"It does."

"And the first name that God gave Moses seems to indicate that," I asserted. "God was saying to Moses that everything is one, and we are all contained in that oneness. Why were the other names needed then?"

"Here's one example from the Kabbalistic Zohar (the Book of Splendor). It relates the story of the 2nd-century Talmudic sage Rabbi Eleazar. He lived with his father, another well-known rabbi named Rabbi Simeon, whom I've mentioned earlier. One day, he asked his father to explain the words *Ehyeh Asher Ehyeh*. Rabbi Simeon answered by saying, 'Eleazar, my son, behold. Everything is bound together in one thing, and the mystery of the thing is Ehyeh Asher Ehyeh. It includes everything . . . the sum of all, hidden and not revealed.' You see, *Ehyeh* is identified in Kabbalah as the foremost of the Sacred Names of God.

"Then in the 12th century, Maimonides, author of *The Guide for the Perplexed,* came along. He talked about something called 'the perfect Unity of God' and tried to reconcile the many Divine Names in the Old Testament with what he considered to be that perfect unity. He believed that YHWH (also known as the Tetragrammaton), was the only proper name of God. He considered *Ehyeh Asher Ehyeh,* along with *Yah* (another Divine appellation meaning 'eternal existence'), to be the explanation of the name YHWH. So even within the corpus of Kabbalistic thought and works, there are different interpretations and ways to comprehend this, but eventually, it all leads back to the understanding of ourselves as Divine Holy Sparks in search of Divine Union, or *Hieros Gammos*—the ultimate marriage of our human and Divine natures . . . our perfect relationship with God."

"Phil, you've mentioned that there are many names of God from a Kabbalistic perspective, but you also said that the Tetragrammaton—the I AM—is the highest. Do all of the other names derive from the first?"

"While it may be true that all names are contained within the Most Holy Name, certain names are keys that open gates within us, allowing grace in the form of Divine qualities or attributes to flow into us and through us into the world of form. The irony is that we already possess these Divine qualities; they just need to be brought back into our awareness."

"You also told me that the next part of the journey is to learn how to use the different names to achieve power," I added.

"That's not what I said at all," Phil maintained, shifting his mood almost instantly. "The names of God aren't meant to be used to achieve power, at least not power for its own sake. That's an improper use of it, to say the least . . . not to mention potentially dangerous. There have been misguided individuals and groups throughout time that have tried. Using the Holy Names as a means of gaining power for yourself and not for the benefit of others always leads you in the wrong direction. It's the ego's way, not the soul's. As I said, the Kabbalistic understanding of the ego is the will to receive pleasure, but with the intention to only please oneself. This, in large part, is what constituted the original Fall from Grace. What we're seeking here is to use the different names to receive grace that can be of benefit to all beings. I told you that we have a mission together, but it isn't about achieving power."

Phil's words were sharper than he likely intended. I didn't mean to imply that we were about to use the power he spoke of simply for ourselves. He seemed to realize this and relaxed in his seat. "I'm sorry I came on so strong," he said, turning his face away from me. "This is pretty serious stuff, and if we're going to succeed, I need to make sure you have the right intention—what's called *kavanah*."

"I don't even know what my intention is because I'm not exactly sure what we're talking about," I confessed.

"You'll understand soon enough. It's all going to become very clear in the next few days."

"What do you mean?"

"You don't think I came all the way here simply to give you a crash course in Kabbalah, do you?" Phil turned back toward me, smiling. "You already know where we're going. We're going to Paris. That's where the work needs to be done."

"What kind of work are you talking about?"

"It is said that the Divine Names are vehicles of revelation, personal revelation, for it's through the proper use of the names that gates will open within you that will allow the presence of God to manifest through you. And when you master the name, you master the spiritual force that is manifested through that particular name. Jimmy, you can become what the ancients called the *Ba'alei Shem,* a 'Master of the Name,' but first you must master your own name."

"What do you mean, 'master my own name'?"

"The work you've been doing with the Moses Code has helped open people up to a new level of revelation for the benefit of all humanity. Paris is one of the most magical cities in the world. I'm told there are opportunities available at this particular time that don't exist anywhere else on Earth. What I can tell you is that we'll be guided on our journey by a special group of spiritual warriors."

"Spiritual warriors?" I blurted out in a high-pitched tone of voice. "You've got to tell me more. This is really getting interesting."

"Yes, it is. I'm talking about the Knights Templar. Among the treasures they found during their excavations below the Temple Mount back in the 12th century in Jerusalem were architectural plans."

"Architectural plans?"

"Blueprints, more specifically, by which the masons of the time built sophisticated structures, including the Gothic cathedrals, for example. These temples of Divine science were built to resonate with certain forms of consciousness. One of the functions of these energetic structures was to attract and contain certain forms of sentient intelligence, which I believe were never meant to wander the earth freely. This was a holy enterprise, I assure you. The intention was certainly honorable, but sometimes the best-laid plans of mice and men . . . well, let's just say that some consequences were unforeseen."

"The angels and demons you spoke of."

"Yeah, but not quite the way you think. We're not going to Paris to battle demons or dance with angels, or vice versa, for that matter. The reason is for something very different and much more important."

There was a long pause. "What is it?" I asked.

"That's still undecided. There's one more sign I'm waiting for. When it comes, we'll both know."

"Another sign?"

"Yes, something that should confirm what will happen next. I'm not exactly sure what it will be or how it will play out. It may come in a form different from what either one of us might imagine. You think we're going to Paris to release the demons and angels, but that isn't it at all. Using the Sacred Names, which we will do, in reality frees the will and releases you, not them. The names open seals within you that allow grace to flow into and through you into the world, creating a field of love that has the potential to release everyone and everything that comes in contact with it. I've always believed that the chanting of Sacred Names creates literal tunnels—wormholes—in the fabric of space-time. And it's through these pathways that the breath of the Holy Spirit, which exists in the world of fantasy and imagination, can be bridged into this world."

"A bridge from Heaven to Earth."

"Yes, one could say that." Phil continued, "It's more accurate to say from Earth to Heaven. That's what Kabbalah, our work, and, in fact, all works of higher calling are all about: bridge building. Each name we call upon will be like another rung in the ladder . . . a stairway to Heaven, if you will. And if we build this bridge correctly and with enough integrity, then a door will be opened between dimensions, allowing all of us to pass into a brave new world, a world of expanded possibilities, of love that knows no earthly bounds. It all begins in Paris, but there's no way for us to know where it will ultimately lead."

The train seemed to pick up speed for a moment, just as the momentum of our journey was building. There was no way to stop or reverse what had been started. Whatever awaited us in Paris, whether angelic or demonic or both, there was nowhere else to go but forward.

CHAPTER 4

The Other World

The street gutter was filled with raw sewage and odors I hoped I'd never smell again. A group of small Indian children, ranging in age from around five to ten, ran past me laughing, kicking a dirty ball. Their happiness felt strange in this environment, as if it would have been more appropriate for them to be walking with their heads bowed in shame given the terrible conditions. An old woman who must have been at least 80 stepped out from behind a battered door and shook a worn rug in the air, sending dust and dirt flying in every direction. I had to cover my face to keep from inhaling the filth as I stepped to the other side of the street. I didn't see the middle-aged man who was walking behind me, and he swerved to the right as I interrupted his path. He turned and smiled as if nothing had happened.

"I'm sorry . . . excuse me," I said to him.

"Namaste," he answered, as he brought his hands together into a praying position, and then continued walking and smiling.

I saw a small temple ahead and instinctively knew it was my destination. That was also the moment I realized I was dreaming. I was in India, yet it didn't seem at all unusual or strange to be there. I was going to a meeting of some sort, but with whom and why? I also had the sensation that this was more than a dream, as if there were some hidden purpose or reason for my being there. My pace quickened as I approached the temple, and I somehow knew that the answers to all my questions lay within.

Three rats ran through a hole in the wall as I came to the door. It sent a terrible chill up my spine and made me even more cautious and alert. The door was much more ornate than I'd expected, with wood carvings of Hindu gods I didn't recognize. Three of the figures seemed locked in some kind of tantric embrace, as monkeys watched from behind pillars and trees. The other gods sat on the ground in meditation, oblivious to the amorous behavior of their fellows. I reached out and touched the door, feeling the rough wood and centuries-old bas-relief. Although my touch was light, the door began to slowly open as if hung on perfectly oiled hinges.

The smell of sweet incense immediately enveloped me, drawing me forward into the dark entryway. I felt as if there were a magnet that had taken hold of my body, pulling me farther inside, and I had no choice but to place one foot in front of the other. After a slight turn to the left, I realized that I was in the main temple hall, and the sight filled me with awe. The altar was completely covered in the most colorful flowers I had ever seen, and bronze statues from every religion lined the walls. There seemed to be many altars instead of one—one for each statue. My attention was immediately drawn to the bronze Blessed Mother, and I saw the tiny figure of a nun kneeling in prayer, her head bowed so I couldn't see her face. I tried to walk as quietly as I could to avoid disturbing her, but the floorboards betrayed me with a loud creak that echoed through the room.

"I've been waiting for you," a voice said. I wasn't sure at first, but the voice seemed to come from the nun. She had a distinct accent but hadn't said enough for me to be able to place it. Yet there was something familiar about her, as if I knew this holy woman, although I didn't know how.

"You've been waiting for me?" I asked in a low voice.

The nun spoke as she gathered her strength to stand. "Of course. Why else would I be here?" At that moment I saw her face, and my breath left my lungs.

"Mother Teresa?!" I exclaimed in disbelief. "Why are you here . . . why have you been waiting for me?"

She took three steps in my direction, and then almost miraculously, she was suddenly standing right in front of me. "We need to talk." She reached out for my hand, guiding me to the corner where a long bench sat against the wall. She motioned for me to sit on one side and she sat on the other. "There is some information you need, and I wanted to be the one who told you."

"Information?" I asked, trying to process what was happening.

"Yes . . . essential information. You're about to go on a journey that has the potential to either more clearly define your soul's purpose or destroy you from within. There are powerful allies on your side, but there are also adversaries. You have to learn how to recognize which is which, to know those who are sent to guide you and those who are meant to distract."

"Mother, I'm so glad you're here and that you want to help me in this way, but I don't know what you mean. Are you saying that this journey I'm on with Phil is dangerous? Is someone trying to stop us?"

"Not someone," she answered in a serious voice. "Something. You're going to encounter forces that you've never seen or known about before. These forces do not mean you any harm. They simply want to continue to protect what they have always guarded. You are the one who might steal it away, and the force knows that. That's why I'm here—to tell you how to protect yourself."

Her words filled me with dread, and although I knew I was dreaming, I also felt something very real, as if what she was telling me might save my life. "What do you mean by the forces and that they want to protect what they've always guarded?"

"There are energies—that's the best way I have of describing them—that are afraid of the light because they believe they are outside of the loving care of eternity. They'll do anything to continue hiding because they're convinced that they'll be punished if they're finally exposed. What you're considering doing will reveal where they're hiding, and they may lash out because of it."

"I'm not even sure what you're talking about, so it's hard for me to know what to do."

Mother smiled and took my hand again. "Your love will be your shield. Your light and your intention will ultimately guide you, and that's what I'm here to tell you. Trust your light, and let your love guide every step and every action. If you do, then you'll be invulnerable. But if you become afraid, your light will dim and you'll be helpless. Then they may attack, and you will be lost."

"This is about Paris," I said, suddenly remembering where I would find myself when I woke up.

"It is about you, and it is about why you're in Paris." She stood up. "Please remember what I told you. Don't be afraid no matter what might happen. Let your love guide your path, and everything will unfold as it should."

She started to walk back toward the statue where I found her praying. "Mother . . ." I called, but she seemed to disappear through a small door I hadn't seen just behind the statue. I stood up and wondered what I was supposed to do next.

I was standing in the same spot when seconds later, a young boy, one of the children I'd seen earlier kicking the ball down the street, ran into the temple. "Mister, come with me now. Please hurry!" He grabbed my hand and pulled me out the door into the bright sunlight. He was pulling almost faster than I could run, as we turned off the street and darted down a small alley. Others shot past, running away from whatever we were running toward. There was panic everywhere; I wondered where we were going and why.

"Come, before it's too late!" the boy exclaimed, as we ran inside a building, and then up a single flight of stairs. My senses were confronted with a wide range of strange smells, from curry to burning wood. I wondered if the house was on fire, which would explain why the others were running away from the scene. We finally arrived at a door, and the boy pushed it open. At first I saw several women crying and rocking back and forth; then one of them noticed us and turned around. When she did, I saw what they were all focused on. A woman, perhaps in her mid-20s, was lying on a small cot in the midst of labor, sweat rolling down her thin face. Something was wrong, which explained why the others were weeping. The woman who first saw us quickly came toward me and took my hand from the boy. "Come . . . please, do something to help her!"

Before I knew it, I was next to the cot, and the pregnant woman looked up at me with desperate eyes. She was naked, and her belly seemed to rise and fall as she breathed, and it struck me as terribly abnormal. The others kept pointing toward the young woman and pleading with me. "What should I do?" I asked. "I don't know what's happening."

The boy stepped into the group. "Help her to bring the baby. You're the one who was sent to us. You must help her give birth to the child."

"But why? What am I supposed to do? I don't have any idea how to do this!"

"Trust what you know," the pregnant woman said softly through her heavy breathing. Her voice was frail; it seemed to take tremendous effort for her to speak. "The light will guide you . . . you will know."

Sweat began pouring down my face, and I could feel my knees beginning to buckle. I didn't understand what she meant and had no idea what they expected me to do. The young woman took my hand and placed it on her round belly. I instantly felt the child in her womb pushing against my hand, straining to be released. "Trust what you already know," she whispered.

I took a deep breath and let my hand move over the surface of her skin, hoping that something would come to me. Nothing. I looked over at the boy and he smiled, and for just a moment, my confusion lifted. I leaned forward and put my mouth near her midsection. At first, I wasn't sure what I was about to do, but then it all became perfectly clear. I opened my mouth and let the words flow: "*Ehyeh Asher, Ehyeh,*" I softly spoke. "*Ehyeh Asher, Ehyeh.* I AM THAT, I AM. I AM THAT, I AM . . ."

I chanted the phrase over and over until the movement in her belly finally began to relax. Then there was a sudden rush of movement, like air being released from a balloon. "It's working . . .

it's working!" the boy shouted, and a look of profound relief washed over the young woman's face. Then I heard the sound of a baby crying, and I looked down to see one of the older women wiping the afterbirth off the infant. The other women began crying even louder, but now their tears were filled with joy.

The boy took me by the hand again and led me away from the cot. "I told them you would do it! I knew you would be able to help her."

"What just happened?" I asked him.

"What do you mean? The child is now alive. It is because you were there . . . there was no other way it could happen."

"Yes, I know I was there, but I still don't know what I did. The name of God came to me so I started chanting it. Then I felt the energy, and it swept through her. But why did I have to do it? Why couldn't you or any of the other women?"

"I don't know what you mean," he said, "but the holy man might."

"What man are you talking about?"

"Come, I will show you."

He took my arm and we left the room. I looked over at the young woman who was now holding her baby close to her chest as the others were lovingly stroking them both. We walked through the hallway and down the stairs. Seconds later we were outside again, but it was no longer India. We were in a desert. The sun was blinding, and I had to cover my eyes. I could hear voices in the distance—male voices speaking in a language I didn't understand, although it sounded Semitic, perhaps Hebrew or Arabic. When my vision adjusted, I saw that I was just outside what looked to be an outdoor bazaar of some sort. I could see merchants displaying their wares under tents billowing under a soft breeze. The scent of perfumes and something else entered my nostrils. I spun around and found myself face-to-face with a camel. The boy was gone.

I walked toward the marketplace. Realizing that I was thirsty, I looked around for something to drink. A voice from behind startled me. "You are early." I turned to find an elderly Jewish man, his bright eyes beaming at me. His smile was visible under a long black beard speckled with gray. He had what looked like a white prayer shawl wrapped around his shoulders.

"Where am I?" I asked, feeling a little disoriented.

"You are in the holy city of Jerusalem. How could you not know where you are? I was told you were a man of intelligence."

I was trying to figure out what was happening. "And who are you?"

"My name is Eleazar. Eleazar ben Durdia. You may call me rabbi, although I wasn't fortunate enough to have that distinction while I was alive—no matter. I've come to explain things to you, to help you understand."

"What do I need to understand?"

"First, you must share with me what you have learned thus far. But please, my manners. Come sit down here, and we will have some tea."

I looked behind us and spied a circular wooden table set very close to the ground and surrounded by brightly colored pillows propped up on worn rugs. We each sat on a pillow, after which a man approached the table. Eleazar whispered something in his ear, and the man disappeared into a crowd of people.

"You want me to tell you what I've learned so far?" I asked. "That's a very big question, and I'm not sure where to begin."

"Begin at the beginning," he replied. "That's a logical place to start—wouldn't you agree? Tell me what you know about the name."

"*The* name?"

"Yes, *Ha Shem*—or more pointedly, *Shem ha-Meforesh*, 'the Name of Names.'"

"Do you mean the Holy Name?" I asked.

"All names are holy. The one you believe is the holiest, yes. Tell me what you believe."

I waited for a moment, hoping that some direction, some Divine inspiration, would enlighten me. After a while, he looked at me as if he were beginning to grow impatient. "Okay, I know there are many names, but the first name God gave Moses, *Ehyeh Asher Ehyeh*, must be the most important, right?"

"Yuh," Eleazar grunted. "Your pronunciation is terrible; nonetheless, what do you think God meant when he revealed his name?"

"He was telling Moses that Divinity is contained within all things, and therefore, all things are Divine."

"Oy vez mir!" Eleazar shook his head and looked up at the sky. "For saying that, you would surely be branded a heretic. You cannot have unity with the Divine while here on Earth . . . or so they say." For a moment, the twinkle in his eye reminded me of Phil. "Here, it is believed that God is God and man is man. The two are separate and not equal." But then he leaned toward me and smiled. "At least that is what is taught. Then again, who can truly penetrate the mind of God? Neither you nor I. The will of God is unknowable. God veiled his eternal light in order for the world to come into existence, but man has the capacity within to discover his Source and the meaning and purpose of his creation."

"Which is—"

"To return from a state of exile in the lower worlds," he said in a dramatic voice. "But I get ahead of myself. We are all God's Holy Sparks who are seeking redemption. At the time of Tikkun, God's Holy Sparks will return to the unity from which they fell before the creation of the world. This is what is taught in Kabbalah, and it is the hope of man. Look at me. I was one of the greatest sinners ever known. It has been said that there was not a single prostitute I did not sleep with. How little is understood. I asked for Divine Mercy and cried myself to death; and through my death, grace was conferred upon me.

"This does not have to be your way. Let the scholars and academics debate the usefulness of my death and the lesson of my life. Your friend will tell you more. I turned back toward grace, and so will you. It will lead you to the union you so desire. I do not know for sure, but I can hope."

"We can all hope, rabbi," I affirmed. "I hope that I'm finally going to understand what this dream is all about. I keep moving from one scene to another, and they don't seem to make any sense."

"Oh, but they do make sense, my son. Think about it . . . each part brought out a different quality in you and taught you a lesson. The nun from Calcutta told you that—"

"That love would be my shield."

"Yes, very good. And the mother in labor. You helped her . . ."

"By chanting the Holy Name."

"And now that you are here with me. What do you think this is for?"

"I really have no idea."

"Think, my son. There is a cord that binds them all together—it's the essence of all three parts."

I thought about it for a moment and asked myself, *What does Mother Teresa represent? Unconditional compassion, service, love. And the young woman in labor? She was dying. I chanted the name over her unborn child, and the child was born without pain.* "I would say grace. That's the experience at the center of each one. Even now, sitting here with you."

"And what does this grace tell you?"

I didn't know where my next thoughts came from. They didn't even seem to come from my mind, but from somewhere far away from me . . . yet they felt true, even though I still didn't completely comprehend what they meant. "Grace tells me that all is in Divine Order. It tells me that even though things seem to be out of balance, and even dangerously close to disaster, God's will is being done perfectly at this and every moment."

"It is all contained in the *Ehyeh,* in the I AM," Rabbi Eleazar confirmed. "God claims every moment and situation, every person and every being, whether angelic or demonic. All is contained in God, just as you said earlier. You must remember this. No matter what may transpire, you must always remind yourself that, as you would say, God is the center. We cannot yet fully understand the infinity of God because God restricted its light so that creation could take place. But know that God is the center and the center is everywhere. Remember that, and nothing can harm you."

"Am I in some kind of danger? Is that what you're suggesting?"

"What is danger? I can tell you that nothing can happen to you that can separate you from who you are. I can tell you that you must be courageous, like a warrior going off to battle in a foreign land. Things are going to happen, yes, but I cannot explain further, for you cannot yet understand. You may not even comprehend them while they are transpiring, but you will know, even in the moment, that God is at the center. Hold on to this, and you will be fine."

"I'm becoming afraid," I confessed.

"I know you are, my son, but there are powerful allies who will assist you, just as the Calcutta saint said. The one who was sent to you will know what to do. I have come to him as well, although he does not remember. I will come to you again. We will meet here. And remember, there is a Torah that is still invisible to the eyes of man. Follow the trail of your Yud, and it will show you how the beginning and ending are joined. In the meantime, listen to him and do whatever he asks, no matter how it may seem."

"Do you mean Phil?"

But the dream was beginning to fade. I could feel the table where we were sitting dissolve into the recesses of my imagination. Seconds later, I sat straight up in my bed.

✡✡✡✡✡

CHAPTER 5

Kabbalah and Crepes

The morning sun streamed in through the bedroom windows, and the sounds from the street outside made it difficult to drift off again. I gazed around the room and my eyes landed on a strange painting of a middle-aged man being impaled by a long spear that was held by a woman with blood pouring from her eyes. It took me several seconds to realize where I was—the apartment Phil had rented for us in the heart of the Parisian district known as Montmartre, which is home to the famous Moulin Rouge cabaret. The apartment was filled with some of the most unusual and grotesque paintings and photographs I'd ever seen, as well as bizarre, sexually charged sculptures by the brother of the woman who owned the place.

I was in a tiny bedroom and could hear Phil in the other room. It sounded like he was on the phone speaking to his girlfriend, Sharmiila, in Australia. I was also surprised when I realized that the details of my dream were so strongly etched in my mind. They seemed immune to the gentle memory drift that accompanies most of my dreams, which quickly fade into the realm of mysterious images and symbols the moment I wake up. But my recollection of the conversations I had with Mother Teresa, the young boy, and

Rabbi Eleazar was as solid as granite; and I knew I should tell Phil about them right away.

"Good morning," I said as I walked into the room. He had just hung up the phone and was pouring some green concoction I didn't want to know much about into a cup.

"How did you sleep?" There was something about the way he asked that made me wonder if he already knew the answer. I'd stopped trying to figure Phil out years ago. His unusual and often unpredictable style made that particularly challenging.

"I'm not really sure. I think I slept well, but my dream . . ."

"Good! That's what I was hoping. Tell me about it."

I explained everything in as much detail as I could. Phil listened as I spoke of the temple and my meeting with Mother Teresa. Then I told him about the woman giving birth and all the strange details of the house and the people there. Before I got to the story of the rabbi, he stopped me.

"Would you like me to tell you the rest?" he asked.

I was shocked. "Can you? Did you have the same dream?"

"Yes and no," he replied. "You were in a marketplace or something in an ancient-looking city in the desert, I think. Then you were in some kind of café. Inside, I could see these little tables that were very low to the ground surrounded by beautiful pillows. You were sitting with an old man, a rabbi, I believe."

"Yes, that's all correct. And what about what he told me?"

"I have no idea what the two of you said to each other," he explained. "I saw the whole scene from across the street. It felt as if I were fixed there and couldn't move. I'm not sure why, but I remember thinking that I had somehow entered into your dream."

"That's amazing! But you couldn't come up to us?"

"No. I saw you both sitting there talking, but no matter what I did, I couldn't move any closer . . . I was frozen there. What did the old man say to you?"

I told him about Rabbi Eleazar and everything I learned. "He's a pretty interesting guy. Is it true that he was a notorious patron of local prostitutes?"

"He was beyond interesting," Phil said as he took a sip of his drink, leaving a thin green line on his upper lip. "Eleazar ben Durdia was considered a great sinner. His repentance at the end of his life earned him a place in the world to come. He cried himself to death, and it was what helped him achieve the grace he longed for. He was awarded the title of rabbi only after his death because of the great lesson he taught us."

"Do you know what that is?"

"The lesson is that each and every one of us is worthy of redemption—in Hebrew, it's called *teshuva,* meaning 'returning to God.'"

"He said that everything we'll do is contained in the first name God gave Moses, *Ehyeh Asher Ehyeh.* We spoke about Paris and that there was something you and I have to do here. He also seemed to believe that we need to be mindful because there are potential dangers involved—just like you said—but the name would protect us."

"The *names,*" Phil stated matter-of-factly.

"What do you mean?"

"Not just one name but ten that correspond to the Sephiroth, or Divine Emanations of the Kabbalistic Tree of Life. *Ehyeh Asher Ehyeh* is certainly one, perhaps the most important, but the others will be essential as well. I think this is the sign I was waiting for, signifying that we're on the right track."

"So, you already knew what we're going to do?" I inquired.

"I had an idea," he said, "but I also knew that something had to come along to confirm what I had long suspected, or thought I knew. That's what your dream has done. Everything Mother Teresa said to you was dead-on. She talked about the allies and the adversaries that we might encounter on our little journey here in Paris. There will be those who will want to see this work done and others who will try to stop it. They oppose it because they're afraid of what it might mean or where it might leave them. Those who live in the world of shadows are always afraid of the light even though it can set them free. She also said that our greatest defense would be love, and that we should never lose faith in that."

"What about the woman giving birth?" I asked him.

"The woman giving birth is also highly significant. There is a great birth—rather, a *rebirth* that's taking place in the world right now, but the labor pains of this new birth may seem overwhelming. Sometimes it feels like we're all going to perish—that humanity won't make it through this transitional phase. We try to hold back because we don't want to change. We're in the most critical period in our tenure here as embodied souls. We've got to change if we want to continue evolving, but it's a very scary proposal for many people to consider because they don't know what awaits them on the other side. However, there's one thing that has the potential to gently facilitate our passage into this next Golden Age."

"The names of God?" I offered.

"More like the presence of God, which is certainly invoked when one correctly uses the names of God. Once again, the work we're here to do won't be accomplished through the use of one name, but *ten*. There are numerous Sacred Names that all represent the different aspects of Divinity. As Rabbi Simeon explained, everything is bound together in one thing, and that thing is *Ehyeh*. It is one of the names we'll be using, but there are others that reflect additional Divine qualities or aspects of the Creative Fire. Maybe it's time for me to tell you exactly what we're going to do over the next couple of days."

"Yes!" I exclaimed, with a deep sigh of relief. "I think that's a great idea."

"I'm not sure how to best describe all this, but everything tells me that this is the perfect place for us to be right now. There's no other city in the world that has as much as Paris can offer, at least in terms of what we're about to attempt. I've heard that the Goddess Isis is the protectress of Paris and that the word *Paris* comes from *Para Isidos,* which means 'near the Temple of Isis.'"

"Is there a temple of Isis near Paris?" I asked.

"Well, since you mention it, a statue of Isis is said to have once stood on the site that is now the Church of Saint-Germain-des-Prés."

"Why doesn't it surprise me that you knew that?"

"Surprise is a wonderful experience, though. Wouldn't you agree?"

"How long have you been studying this?" I asked, ignoring his question.

"Longer than I should probably say."

"Okay. Then tell me what we're doing here."

Phil sat down in a chair across from me and took a deep breath. I could tell he was about to reveal the whole purpose or reason for our journey, as if everything led to this moment. It seemed like the adventure was finally about to begin. "All right. I know this is the moment you've been waiting for, so let's get down to it. There are specific locations throughout Paris—churches, cathedrals, even a park—where certain energies are trapped . . . you might even say held hostage. In some cases, they're trapped because horrible events took place there; in others, it's because that was the intent of the builders, as I started to tell you on the train on the way here, remember?"

"Yeah. Keep going."

❧ "Okay. Remember when I told you that the geometric architecture of many of these structures either purposely or inadvertently imprisoned certain forces and have kept them contained until they could be safely sent back to where they rightfully belong?"

"You're losing me."

"Do you remember what I said about the Knights Templar and the secrets they were rumored to have had?"

"I don't know what the secrets are, but yes, I've heard that and also remember you'd mentioned them. Go on."

"Some of those secrets have been encoded into the geometry of the churches and cathedrals that were built using the plans that the Templars provided, many of which are right here in Paris."

"What were these secrets meant to do, and why are they there?"

"Well, powerful wave patterns, or standing wave fields, that are generated by certain symbol codes embedded in the architecture of these sites act like tractor beams that attract or grab onto specific discarnate entities and hold them. To use a crude but simple example—"

"Like a moth to a flame?"

"I was thinking more like an insect trap that puts out a particular scent or even sound. You fly all the time, Jimmy. You must have seen these types of things advertised in *SkyMall* magazine, right?"

"I'm not usually looking for a better mousetrap," I said, smiling.

"Or a mousetrap, now that you mention it! The scent of the cheese 'grabs' the mouse, and it has no choice but to move toward it. It works pretty much the same way with these entities. When a particular entity, or intelligence, resonates with a particular geometric symbol or code, it can't help but be pulled in. And once it's in, it can be trapped for centuries, sometimes millennia, and even eons. That's when things get really hairy."

"You mean it gets even stranger?" I asked, trying to lighten the air a bit.

"Much stranger." Phil continued, "In some cases, the trapped entities will literally take up residence, exerting tremendous influence, which distorts the original purpose of the place. And sometimes, they even take complete control."

"I think I'm beginning to understand what you're saying. Say there's a cathedral that was built in honor of the Blessed Mother, and let's assume that the geometric architecture of the place traps some kind of spirit or entity or, as you might say, dimensionalized consciousness. Then they set up shop there and think it's their home. People come to the church to pray or sightsee and may encounter the spirit without even realizing it. I think I've actually heard of this before or maybe read it somewhere."

"Sometimes it's just a vibe that someone picks up. I'm sure you've experienced this yourself on occasion."

"Are they all negative spirits?" I asked.

"Not at all!" Phil laughed. "Some of them are very positive, extremely benevolent angelic presences. But if they're unable to leave, they can't fulfill their soul's purpose. At the same time, being trapped there interferes with the purpose of the place, the church, or wherever it might be, not to mention those charged with their stewardship, if you get my drift. Being in such close proximity to certain energies can and does have a corrupting influence. That's why intervention is sometimes required to help them all move on and be released."

"It sounds like some kind of geometric exorcism—"

"No, Jimmy," Phil snapped back. "At least not in the way you might imagine. You've seen the movie *The Exorcist,* haven't you?"

"Yeah . . . the scariest movie ever made."

"Well, do you remember what the priests say over and over when they're conducting the ritual?"

"I think it's something like 'The spirit of Christ compels you . . . the power of Christ . . .'"

"Yeah, yeah!" Phil burst out, becoming even more excited. "And what is the power of Christ, or God, and where do you think that power is concentrated?"

I thought for a moment, not exactly sure where he was leading me. "I would say it can be found in the name of God, like *Ehyeh Asher Ehyeh.*"

"Correct. So the power of God—which in the final analysis is what an exorcist might use to release a demonic spirit, for example—can be found in one or more of the many names of God. In fact, many of the rituals of exorcism use various holy names to release so-called demons. Usually, it's 'In the name of the Holy Spirit' or 'In the name of so and so.' You see, using the names, or rather, the *power* of the names, is very tricky business. That's why actual names were seldom used."

"I don't know much about exorcism, but it seems to make sense. If the name of God has the power to create worlds or produce miracles, then it can do anything."

"And that's what we're going to do."

"What do you mean?"

"The ten spots in Paris that we'll be visiting on this journey have been part of an ongoing investigation of mine for several years—many are Templar in origin or design, or they have some kind of Templar connection. The Templars are important because they held so much power in their time and controlled so many secrets. That gave them worldly as well as occult power, and for the most part, they wielded their power with cunning and intelligence. But, as sometimes happens, things went in a different direction, or at least there were unanticipated results. The Templars probably could have rectified it all, but they're no longer here. The church wiped them out, or so we've been told. But we're here now, and we're going to finish the job."

"What job are we going to finish?" I asked. "Are we going to play 'ghostbuster' to the spirits of Paris?"

"Something like that." Phil smiled. "It may seem like I'm being a little overdramatic, but I'm serious. We're going to use some very powerful names to help release energies that have been trapped at these locations—some for a very long time—so they can finally fulfill their destinies. The result could be greater than either of us can imagine, both for the locations themselves and for the world at large."

"So, we're going to run around Paris doing some kind of bizarre rituals in all these different places?" I inquired, almost as if it were all a joke.

"Bizarre? No. But yes, that's pretty much it," Phil affirmed.

"But won't it look strange? We can't just walk in and start waving incense in the air and speaking in tongues. This is starting to sound crazy, even for you."

"'Crazy is as crazy does,' as Forrest Gump might say. It may sound crazy, I'll admit, but it's why we're both here. We're not in Paris to go to the top of the Eiffel Tower; we're here to do something that could have a dramatic impact on the whole world. We're going to attempt to undo some horrible wrongs by using the most powerful force in history: the presence of God. I'm sorry if there was something else you had in mind, like sightseeing or something, but this is why we're here."

"You have to admit that it all sounds bizarre," I said to him.

"It's no more bizarre than anything else we've seen in our travels. Just think about it: if we're successful, we could help facilitate some amazing transformations, within ourselves and the world. I'm talking about some pretty miraculous stuff."

"And if we're not?"

"To be honest, I really haven't considered that possibility." Phil sat farther back in his seat.

"Maybe we *should* think about it. What do you think would happen?"

"Well, it's hard to say. I guess it's possible that it could all blow up in our faces."

"What does that mean?" I was getting nervous. "What would that look like?"

"There's no telling. . . . I said earlier that some of these entities have been trapped for centuries, possibly eons. We're going to be focusing a tremendous amount of light in their direction."

"You're scaring me again."

"Don't be scared. Like Mother Teresa said, love will be our shield—and theirs. We can surely trust that we'll be protected."

"I can only hope you're right."

"Yes, you and me both." Phil stood up from the chair. "You know, only one thing didn't escape from Pandora's box. Do you want to know what it was?"

"I know this one," I said. "It was hope."

"Correct. 'Hope springs eternal.' So, are you ready?"

"Ready for what?"

"Are you ready to begin? There's no reason to wait. I say we start moving toward the first location."

"You're not one to waste time," I replied. "What about preparation or tools?"

"And what tools would you recommend?"

"I don't have any idea! This is my first time."

"Mine, too."

Phil said those words just as I was standing up from my chair, and I felt as if I were about to lose my balance. "Are you kidding me?!" I nearly screamed. "You've never done this before?"

"To my knowledge, what we're going to attempt has never been tried before, at least not since the creation of the world. That's what makes it so exciting."

He was up and running out the door before I knew what was happening. "Where are we going?" I asked.

He stopped and turned around. "Lots of places—but not until we've had crepes. We can't make another move without first tweaking our taste buds."

"Why? There can't be any deep, mystical reason for eating crepes before exorcising the churches and cathedrals of Paris. Or is there?"

"Nothing overtly mystical." Phil grinned. "I just love them, and there's no better place for crepes than Paris. For one thing, we can't do this work on empty stomachs, and there's a great place for crepes on the way to where we're going."

"And where is that?"

"After we eat, we're going to one of my favorite spots in Paris—Sacré-Coeur, the Basilica of the Sacred Heart. That's where our adventure will begin."

We walked down the stairs past a gauntlet of fertility and fetish sculptures, portraits of tortured souls and demons, and an even stranger painting of Rhett Butler and Scarlett O'Hara. I tried not to look at any of them, assuming they'd give me the creeps before even starting the work at hand. Within seconds, we were out the door. Phil's pace was brisk, and I nearly jogged to keep up with him. The morning was cold and wet, and Phil pulled his red beret low over his forehead to block the rain. He'd stuffed several notepads and a book in his backpack, and I wondered if they were filled with ancient formulas for battling demonic forces.

"Just around the corner here," he called out over his shoulder. He darted into a small café, and I saw the hot crepe iron through the window. We sat down at a table in the back, and I assumed that this was the spot where he'd prepare me for our first location. Once seated, he took out one of the notepads and opened it to the first page.

"You told me there were ten places we needed to visit," I said once I was in my chair. "Why?"

"You tell me. How did this part of the journey start for you?"

"I'm not sure which part you're referring to."

"When *The Moses Code* was first released, what was the trigger point for all this new inquiry?"

"It was the Yud," I stated. "I realized that the mystery was far deeper than I first thought and had to know more. That's why I contacted you."

"Exactly. And what is the number of the Yud?"

"The number?"

"Yes," he replied dispassionately. "Its position in the Hebrew alphabet—its simple gematrian value. Do you remember what its number is?"

"Yes, I think so. It's ten, isn't it?"

"Yes, of course. That's one reason why we have to visit ten locations. There are other important reasons that will make themselves known as we progress on our journey. Remember that the Yud represents the 'finger that points the way'—the opened and closed hand of God. It's literally the seed of the Tree of Life. It's how Divine Inspiration enters the world. It's the pause between the breath of God and the breath of man. Do you see? The Yud has everything to do with our mission."

"And how are we going to use of the names of God to accomplish whatever it is we're trying to accomplish?" I said these words just as the waitress arrived at our table, and just as suddenly realized how little I knew about our so-called mission. I did know that everything I was feeling inside—perhaps everything I'd experienced in my life up to this point—had led me there. For a minute, though, I wondered if I was crazy for following Phil to Paris, and then agreeing to run around in the rain doing God knows what. He was supposed to be back home getting well. And what about my dream? Was I playing right into some kind of strange delusion?

"We're not going to use the names of God," Phil said once we ordered our crepes. "They're going to use us."

"And how is that?" I asked.

"We're going to become the conduits through which the consciousness of the Divine Names can manifest. We're going to use them to transform from within, like I've said to you earlier, and then the rest will happen on its own."

"Okay." I was still confused. "So we're not going to really do anything but chant the names in the churches?"

"No—much more than that. The names will open a series of tunnels, or wormholes, in the fabric of space-time through which any number of things can happen."

"I'll rephrase my question. How will the names use us?"

"We are to be instruments of peace," he replied, taking a sip of the cappuccino the waitress put in front of him. "How God will manifest through us by the use of the names we cannot fully know. Much is beyond our understanding, but let's talk a little more about the Sacred Names and how we can use them. For the sake of this discussion, there are seven ways to use these Divine Expressions, as suggested by Dr. J. J. Hurtak, a scholar and Orientalist. These are the ways he suggested using the Sacred Names in his book *The Seventy-two Sacred Names of the Myriad Expressions of the Living God.* He also wrote *The Book of Knowledge: The Keys of Enoch.* You have to understand this before we can begin."

Seconds later our crepes arrived, but Phil didn't wait to continue. "First of all, using the Sacred Names initiates a strong link with God, or Divine Father, so that our spiritual identity is connected with the highest of all levels."

"My understanding is that the link has never been severed," I added. "Wouldn't it be more accurate to say that we have to become conscious of the link that is already present?"

"Yes, using the names correctly helps one to be conscious of that eternal connection."

"It's like being on the phone with someone, but if you don't acknowledge the voice or the presence on the other end, there really is no conversation taking place. You have to engage, and once engaged, information can be shared, and that's what we want: a flow of information, of grace. Isn't that what you've been saying?"

"Precisely. The second way Sacred Names can be used is for the advancement of the soul, using them in personal prayer and meditation to open the veils and gates. This is something I'll talk to you about at length as we continue our journey."

"I feel like I should be writing this down," I remarked.

"Don't worry, it will be there when you need it. The third way is to create an active network through which Divine Light can operate. There have always been individuals and communities of Lightworkers in the world throughout time who have done this. You've called them 'Emissaries of Light.'"

"The Emissaries described it in a very similar way," I said to him. "They said that the work they did and the meditations they used created a kind of spiritual fountain that allowed the energy of Divine Light to spread across the earth and touch every living being. It sounds very similar to what you're describing."

"Yes, it is. The fourth and fifth ways the Sacred Names can be used are closely related. They can be used in prayers for healing and for world peace, as well as in times of planetary crisis or need in order to call forth additional light and love. Calling upon the names in that way creates a channel for the healing to occur, but it has to be initiated through us. It affirms our faith in the wisdom of God and that the prayers we send out will be answered according to God's will. Does that make sense?"

"Yes," I affirmed, "totally."

"You can also use the names for the protection of the spiritual and physical garment, which is another way of describing the body of light that we happen to be clothed in at any particular moment. The Divine Names can quite literally build a wall of light, and believe me, that's going to come in handy. On this journey of ours, we're going to encounter various forms of sentient consciousness—both physical and nonphysical—that will be drawn to this light for redemption and reconciliation. However, where there is the greatest light, it can and will attract the greatest darkness, as you well know. That's why it's important that we have the means to protect ourselves, and the proper use of the names is our greatest protection."

"Got it!" I exclaimed, trying to stay involved.

"The final way the Sacred Names can be used is for working directly with the Messengers of the Hierarchy and for the discernment of hierarchies, when they make themselves known to us."

"This one sounds a lot more complicated."

"Not really. Using the names correctly can facilitate direct work with the Angelics, for example. From your perspective, Jimmy, it's the ability to work with these beings and to understand them not with your mind but with your soul. There are forms of sentient consciousness all around us, but that doesn't mean that their will is aligned with God's will, if you get my drift. It's like walking up to someone on the street and asking him for directions to a particular place. Just because he gives you an answer, it doesn't mean you're going to make it to your destination. Some know the way and others don't. Some may know *their* way, but it isn't *your* way. The proper use of the Divine Names will enable you to use more discernment in terms of whom you're dealing with, especially when they make their appearance known, as they undoubtedly will."

"That actually makes sense," I said.

"I'm glad to hear that." Phil continued. "Forgive me for repeating this so often, but it is of the utmost importance that we, and whoever else, use the names with the highest level of integrity and impeccability. They are to be used with reverence and respect for the great teachers and sages who have come before . . . with purity of Spirit and with the appropriate degree of preparation, spiritual maturity, and self-examination. We must be conscious that they are part of a greater whole, the object of which is the continuing reeducation and ultimate redemption of the soul.

"Remember, Jimmy, the geometry and architecture of these temples attract a wide range of spiritual energies, both positive and negative. Chanting the names can sometimes attract, shall we say, less evolved forms of consciousness or spiritual energies. They can be released into the light, though, through the interdimensional channels connecting the worlds that are opening at this most crucial moment in our tenure here as embodied souls."

He was starting to lose me again. "Wait . . . that was a lot all at once. Can you say that one more time in a way I can actually get it?"

"Listen, Jimmy. There are codes and formulas built into the geometrical architecture of many of the places we'll be visiting that were put there intentionally by designers who had a fairly comprehensive but, in some important aspects, limited knowledge of advanced spiritual law and practice. I'll be showing you many of these codes and formulas as we progress. In reality, they're in plain sight at many of the locations we'll be visiting. People look at them every day but have no idea that they're actually interdimensional gateways.

"For example, quite often you'll see a Templar cross or other symbols placed in unusual spots in a church. Sometimes these geomantic codes—or *geomancies* as they're called—are used as energy sources, like batteries, that keep other symbols or symbol codes energized. If we can identify some of these, then we can use the names to release their programs or interrupt an ongoing program. Of course, we do that by first releasing the seals within ourselves. That's the real secret: not to try to do it outside, but to do it on the inside."

"What do these entities do?" I asked. "Are they dangerous or malevolent in nature? If they've been here for centuries, or even thousands of years, as you suggest—"

"Most are not mean-spirited at all," Phil interrupted. "They're simply trapped. Please remember that some of these entities were never meant to wander the earth freely. They were brought to this world by misguided souls who, in their quest for power and riches, invoked these spiritual energies—literally yanked them from their home worlds—to do their bidding. Space and time are overlapping, dimensions are blending, and for the first time in a very long time, doors are opening that will allow these lost souls to return home. It's very similar to people who have passed over but haven't realized that they have died, or souls who are simply not ready to pass over and remain earthbound in their confused state, causing a lot of problems here."

"You mean like poltergeists?"

"Yes, precisely," Phil agreed, straightening himself up and staring me squarely in the eyes. "Then there are the entities, or spiritual forces, that have been placed at many of these locations to guard even more ancient secrets. Let's hope we don't run into any of those."

"What will happen if we do?" I inquired, swallowing hard.

"Let's just hope it doesn't happen. That's another thing about using the names: you have to be open to whatever happens because there's always a higher purpose, although at the time we may not be aware of what it is. We're going to be used as instruments—instruments of peace, a role in which you're not entirely unfamiliar—and we have to know that we're protected on the highest levels."

"We can only hope," I remarked. "I don't want to end up a casualty of the cathedrals of Paris."

Phil smiled, but he looked uneasy. I could tell he was as nervous as I was, as if we were on the first ship attempting to sail to the New World. In theory, we knew what we were about to do. But in practice, anything could happen, including all of the scary possibilities that were racing through my mind that very moment.

✧✧✧✧✧

CHAPTER 6

Sacred Heart Basilica

The Tetragrammaton

The steps that led to Sacred Heart Basilica, Basilique du Sacré-Coeur, were directly across the street from the café. A carousel stood to one side, unused because of the light rain that was falling. We opened our umbrellas and crossed the street, passing several tour groups speaking in different languages as their guides explained the history of the area. Then we mounted the first flight of steps, working our way toward the basilica.

Couples and groups gathered near the entrance as we walked through the crowd and past the huge doors into the church. My eyes adjusted to the dim lighting, and the scent of incense and candles greeted me as we made our way to one of the side altars dominated by a statue of Archangel Michael. Phil motioned for me to sit near the corner where we could talk softly without being heard.

"I want to say a bit more about the architecture of these churches," he said. "As I mentioned earlier, the geometry of these cathedrals, like the Kabbalah, encodes a vast body of knowledge whose ultimate purpose is to engender a closer, more personal relationship with God. Kabbalah's emphasis on sound, vibration, form, and numbers is meant to reveal the processes of creation—the geometrical forms and patterns that mirror and inform the very act of creation and the growth and evolution of all manifest forms in nature. These patterns are re-created in the building and structure of sacred places such as this—the objective being nothing less than the transformation of the human into the God-Man, the ultimate unification with our Divine Source.

"This is something that the Templars were very familiar with. Many of them had a working knowledge of the planetary grid system, as well as the geomagnetic corridors of the planet and the vortices upon which these churches and other sacred sites had been built. It's evident that a good deal of that knowledge went into the actual building of churches like this one."

I was holding a pamphlet in English that I took from a display at the front of the church. "Yes, I understand all that, but it says here in the brochure that the first stone for the basilica wasn't laid until 1875—long after the Templars were gone."

"That's true, but it doesn't mean that their concepts and philosophy weren't integrated into its construction. You see, the Templar masons understood that geometric forms revealed the secrets of how Divinity descends into form, and they passed on that knowledge. They also understood that the misuse of ancient magic created many of the problems we're here to try to remedy. But ultimately, these things are beyond the comprehension of the mind alone. They need to be seen through an integration of the heart and soul."

"Is there an example you can give me?" I asked, lowering my voice.

"One of the things I want you to look for here are Templar crosses. This is one of the signs left behind to show their influence. It's called the cross pattée, or *croix pattée.* It's not like your typical Christian cross. It has arms of equal length that are curved, fluted, or spread out at the ends, but they're closed, not indented like the Maltese cross."

"Wouldn't the equal axis of the cross symbolize the movement of energy between the physical planes of existence (the horizontal) and the movement of energy between the spiritual planes of existence (the vertical)?"

"Exactly," Phil confirmed. "It enables a deeper understanding that is both conscious and unconscious, signifying that you get the meaning on multiple levels. It's been said that the Templar cross represents the union of opposites, the union of male and female, and possibly even the spread of the true Gospel to the four corners of the earth. You can look at the cross and see only the general form, but your soul understands its deeper meaning.

"That's actually just a simple example; there are others that are much more advanced. One is the connection between the Templar cross and the fixed signs of the zodiac (which are Leo, Taurus, Scorpio, and Aquarius) and their relation to the four beasts of the Apocalypse. This has to do with the End of Days, or End Times. But I don't want you to be looking for them with your physical eyes alone. Sense them with your soul, and that's where the deeper lessons will be learned."

"Okay. So tell me what we're going to do now," I said.

"I've chosen particular names of God corresponding to the spheres, or Sephiroth, on the Kabbalistic Tree of Life that I feel resonate with the energy of each location we'll be visiting. I think this all came from a dream, but that's neither here nor there. What we're going to do is to activate the energy of each name and then integrate it through prayer, creating a coherent field—a field of influence, as it were—that I'm hoping will illuminate certain portals through which these energies (that have been held hostage) can find their way home. Then I'm going to send you off on your own to follow your own guidance.

"Remember, Jimmy, it will be through opening your own heart that this field will be created—through the grace that will flow into and through you by the use of the names. Something may happen to you, or nothing at all. I think we just have to trust whatever comes up and know that we're doing our very best."

"You said we're going to do a ritual, right? Will it be discreet so we don't stand out?"

"Don't worry, we're not going to do anything that will draw attention. No one will have any idea what we're doing, at least not consciously. But they *will* feel it, whether they know it or not."

"What about the . . . *others?*" I asked.

"What others? Oh, the angels and demons? You're pretty preoccupied with them, aren't you?"

"Should I be? You're the one who said this could all blow up in our faces. So yes, that makes me a bit preoccupied with it. It's not exactly something I've done before."

"That's probably not true."

"What do you mean?"

"I get the feeling we may have done this before, in one form or other. It's also possible that we may have been responsible for creating this in the first place, and we're here now to make amends, to redeem ourselves. I wonder how many people, especially these days, fully understand the awesome, creative power of their thoughts.

"We're here to use the names of God to open seals within ourselves, to be channels for grace to come into the world. The shift will begin in our own consciousness and vibration. When that happens, it allows the same shift to occur in others. This goes on all the time—for example, do you ever notice that when you're happy and walk into a room filled with grumpy people, your energy may help lift them just because you're there?"

"Or their energy could bring me down. Doesn't it depend on whose is stronger?"

"Well, yes and no," Phil contended. "Much depends on you maintaining your focus when you walk into the room. We're entering into this with much more than simply good intentions. We're entering into this with the inherent grace, power, and energy in these Sacred Names. They are all expressions of elevated and exalted thoughts. Using them like we are will provide a powerful focus for us to unleash tremendous power—the power within ourselves."

"Tell me more about the ritual."

"It's actually very simple. As I've mentioned, I've chosen a different name for each of the spots. For example, the name we'll be using here is one we've spoken of before. It's considered by many—not only those of the Jewish persuasion—to be the most important: the Tetragrammaton. We're going to meditate on the name and then repeat it 12 times. After we do so, we'll recite the words *En Sof.*"

"You've said that phrase earlier. What does it mean again?"

"It literally means 'without end' or 'boundless,'" Phil replied. "We sometimes talk about the light of the *En Sof.* It is said that before the creation of the world, the light of the *En* filled the infinite space. Using it in this way amplifies the light of each Divine Name, magnifying its power and directing even stronger intention into the heart of these sacred expressions."

"And why do we repeat it 12 times?"

"There are lots and lots of reasons to do so. The number 12 has enormous mystical, biblical, occult, and especially geometrical significance. For our purpose here, let's just say that there are 12 primary permutations of the four-lettered name of God—the Tetragrammaton—although in truth, there are far more. That's as good a reason as any, don't you think?"

"Whatever you say, Phil. I'm just following your lead."

Phil showed me a way to count off the numbers by looking at the four fingers from the index finger to the pinky. There are 12 sections to those four fingers, making it easier to count by simply touching each finger section while reciting the names. "After a while, it gets to where you don't even notice that you're counting. This is good because we're trying to take the left brain out of this process as much as possible."

"Is there something that should happen at that point?"

"You'll have to tell me," he stated. "The names we will be working with produce waveforms, or patterns of electromagnetic energy, that are shaped according to the architecture of the church, not to mention the geometric architecture of the thought-forms we generate when we chant the names. Energies and perceptions that are veiled from normal waking consciousness are revealed through chanting the names. The words can actually part the veils like Moses parting the Red Sea, or bring down the walls of Jericho . . . to quote the song, 'It's in the way that you use it.' So to answer your question, quite a lot can happen. It just depends on why you're here and what you're ready for."

I could feel myself craving something I could depend on, or at least an idea or potential I could anticipate. "If you had to guess, what would you say?"

"There are so many possibilities," Phil replied. Then his lips curled into a slight smile. "And besides, if I told you, it would take the surprise out of it."

"Great . . . another surprise. And you haven't done this before, right?"

"Like I said, I honestly don't think anyone has ever done this before, at least not successfully. We're working from things I've pieced together from various traditions and writings. To my knowledge, there's really no precedent for any of this. For the most part, we're wingin' it. The angels understand that."

"That scares the heck out of me!" I exclaimed a bit too loud. A woman in front of us turned around to see what was happening. I turned my head away from her toward Phil. "You throw out all this stuff like you've done it dozens of times. How can you really know what we're up against if—"

"I've already told you that I haven't done anything like this before. And anyway, what difference does it make? We're explorers in a bold new experiment in consciousness. We're going where peacemakers have never gone before. It's not the kind of things they write books about, you know."

"I've personally never read anything about going into Gothic cathedrals to release entities that have been trapped inside Templar architecture," I added, moving uncomfortably in my seat.

"Yes, it's exciting but also a little scary."

"A *little* scary?" My discomfort had reached its height.

"You need to let go of your fear, Jimmy. Remember what Mother Teresa said: there are powerful allies at our side. Especially using the Holy Names as we are . . . it sets up a powerful protective frequency that would be hard for anyone, or anything, to penetrate."

"Okay," I said, relaxing a bit. "Tell me more about what we're going to do after we chant the Sacred Name."

"Well, before we even start, I'll offer up a prayer of protection.

Then after the Name has been chanted, we'll sit in silent meditation for a while. We'll simply see what happens or what feelings we get. I suggest we split up at that point and walk around the cathedral. Try to be aware of anything out of the ordinary. Maybe you can let your eyes scan the different frescoes or artwork in case anything opens there. All in all, there are no set rules, only guidelines. We just have to be open to the moment."

It didn't seem like I had much of a choice. I had come this far and decided that I may as well see where it led. If nothing happened, then so be it. It would just be another wild-goose chase, a "bold experiment in consciousness" as Phil proclaimed. But what if something did happen? We would be in different parts of the church, and I wouldn't have his support if a demon suddenly came alive out of a Renaissance painting and attacked me. The idea almost made me laugh, yet I sat back in the pew and took a deep breath.

"Are you ready?" he asked.

"Yes, I'm ready. Let's do this."

"Okay. Close your eyes for a moment, breathe deeply, and we'll begin with a short meditation. The first Holy Name we're going to invoke is Yahweh, followed by the words *Eloah Va Daath,* which means 'Lord God' or even 'Goddess of Knowledge.' In a way, the name relates to the intelligence of the heart and wisdom of Divine Presence. As I said before, Yahweh, or the Tetragrammaton, is held by many to be the most sacred of all the names of God. The word in Hebrew is *Havayah.* It is the second name that God gave Moses in the book of Exodus, when God said to tell them: 'I AM has sent me to you.' It represents the active principle of the *En* ('boundlessness') here in this world, the world of phenomenal existence. It's the four-lettered name of God (spelled 'Yud Heh Vav Heh') sometimes translated or pronounced as 'Jehovah.'

"It's a name that cannot and must not be taken in vain, for it invokes the very essence of the Godhead. This is why the words *Adonai* or *Elohim* are usually substituted for it. It's said to contain the original vibration behind all manifest existence. If you recall, Maimonides believed that it's the *only* proper name for God, and that is why we use it reverently.

"So here's what we're going to do." Phil continued, "We're going to meditate on the name *Yahweh Eloah Va Daath,* but we're going to vocalize the word *Adonai,* meaning 'Lord.' Does that make sense?"

"No, it doesn't," I replied, confused. "Why are we saying one thing and thinking another? Why can't we just recite the letters 'Yud Heh Vav Heh'? I've heard them being chanted before."

"Because from a strict Jewish perspective, to chant the letters of the name is tantamount to saying the name. You need to trust me on this, Jimmy. This may be the first name we're chanting—and I promise it won't continue to be this complicated—but we need to be extremely respectful, especially with this particular name . . . but just for the time being. You're the one who said you wanted to learn about Kabbalah. If you really want to, this is how."

"Okay. I guess I can relax and follow your lead here."

"I'm glad to hear that. So, once again, we'll focus on the Tetragrammaton, in this case the name *Yahweh Eloah Va Daath,* but we'll vocalize the word *Adonai.* Let's take a few deep breaths and begin."

I did as he asked and took a deep breath. I could feel my soul beginning to expand as I meditated, as if each breath were bringing the name closer to my heart. The sound of Phil's voice seemed far away as he softly spoke, even though he was only a few inches to my right. I continued to take deep cleansing breaths, filling my lungs with as much air as I could.

"Now we'll chant the name 12 times, each time ending with *En Sof,* meaning 'boundless existence,'" Phil said, showing me his open palm. "Continue breathing deeply, and don't forget to focus on the Tetragrammaton."

Then we began: *"Adonai, En Sof; Adonai, En Sof; Adonai, En Sof . . ."* Twelve times we chanted the name, and the feeling of expansion continued, especially as I focused my attention on the four-lettered name 'Yud Heh Vav Heh.' My heart and soul seemed to soar over the church and through the rafters. Although I was still fully conscious of myself sitting there in the pew with Phil, I was also aware of so much more . . . an infinite expanse filled with the infinite name of God. When we finished, we sat for a few moments in silence, and then Phil turned and looked at me.

"Remember, Jimmy, each name represents an aspect of spiritual force, or energy, and their use is ultimately to help us receive complete joy and fulfillment. This is what God desires for us. Now we wait and see what happens."

"What should I do?"

"I can't say . . . just stay open and follow your guidance. Be open to receive. I'm going to just walk around. We'll give it as much time as it takes." Phil stood up and walked away toward the front of the cathedral while I sat there wondering what I should do next. The statue of Michael looked down at me, and his powerful stare seemed to be calling me forward into an experience I hadn't yet realized.

"What should I do?" I whispered under my breath. No answer came, only the sound of people brushing past me to get a better look at the side altar where I was sitting.

A man dressed completely in black pushed through three or four tourists until he stood just beneath Michael. The others walked away annoyed, leaving him there looking up into the archangel's eyes. He seemed to be mumbling something under his breath, but it was either in French or was too low for me to discern. He was unshaven and wore dark sunglasses that hid his eyes. Something about the man seemed out of place and I felt a strong urge to get away from him, so I stood up and started walking toward the front of the church to the altar.

I realized that I was walking against the sea of people who had started their tour on one side of the church and then followed a predesignated path around the back and up the other side. It felt right for me to be walking against the grain, as if the only way I'd be able to see whatever it was I came for was to move counter to the rest. I passed at least four side altars, but none of them seemed to call to me. Just across from the main altar, another smaller section dedicated to the Sacred Heart of Jesus drew my attention, so I stepped closer to have a better look. At first nothing jumped out at me, but then I knelt down thinking I'd look less conspicuous than if I stood there like the rest. The enshrined heart was pierced by 12 swords with a tiny flower at the end of each one. I wondered if there was any significance to the prayer Phil and I just shared, as if the number 12 would somehow unlock a deeper mystery. Nothing happened, and after another minute, I stood up and kept walking against the sea of tourists.

I darted between them, moving from side chapel to side chapel, until I was finally directly behind the main altar. There seemed to be a gap in the tour groups, creating just a moment's space for me to look around without being pushed from one side to the other. The sound echoed off the stone walls, and the ancient smell of long-spent incense and burning candles confronted my senses in a way that was both relaxing and alarming. I suddenly remembered why I was there—that the actual architecture of this sacred cathedral might house the souls of entities trapped between worlds . . . and that *I* would somehow play a role in their release.

It suddenly seemed absurd that I ever believed such a story, and I wondered if it was finally time for me to snap out of my misplaced trust and return to reality. I looked around to see if Phil was watching me or was anywhere to be found. Wave after wave of embarrassment washed over me, and I was seconds away from walking out. Our plan was suddenly a reality, not a concept. Until that moment, we were just having a conversation, and I was trusting Phil's brilliance and far-out ideas like a child. But now that I was actually standing there looking for symbols or signs that would indicate that the church might really be holding the energies of which Phil spoke, the reality came rushing around me like quicksand. It was time to get out, and I didn't want to wait another moment.

"Why am I here? Why am I here?"

The voice startled me, and I looked to my left to see who was mumbling the words. It didn't even strike me as odd that it was in English, not French. There were plenty of tourists walking through the church, and many of them were certainly from English-speaking countries, but there was something different, like it wasn't the English I've known and spoken since I was born. I recognized the words, but there was something strange about the way they sounded, perhaps the accent, that made my skin crawl.

"Why am I here? Why am I here?"

It was the man dressed in black wearing sunglasses that I saw at the statue of Archangel Michael. He was looking up at a statue of St. Peter, who held a set of large skeleton keys, which indicated his role of binding in Heaven what was bound on Earth. The man rocked back and forth as he spoke, seemingly staring at the statue without actually seeing it. His eyes seemed to be focused on something much farther away, something that neither I nor anyone else in the church could see. His left hand also seemed to twitch as if holding something that required constant motion . . . as if he held a phone and was sending text messages to another realm. His dark glasses rested on the bridge of his nose just low enough for me to see his eyes, which were vacant in a way that was impossible to describe.

"Why am I here? And why do you keep coming?"

The change in cadence almost shocked me. It was a startling difference, but one I couldn't really understand. The tone of his voice and even the inflection was the same, but the words seemed to indicate something very intimate. Then he turned toward me, as if seeing me for the first time, and the words he spoke sent a cold chill up my spine. "Why did you come here? Why did you come?"

His glasses seemed to descend a fraction of an inch down the bridge of his nose, revealing his eyes and reflecting the candle light in a new and excruciating way. There didn't seem to be anything behind his eyes, although in other respects, they seemed perfectly natural. He looked directly at me but didn't seem to be looking at me at all. It was more of a sensation than a real observation, but it made me feel like running.

Then he stopped, but his eyes continued their blank stare. "I'm sorry," I finally replied. "Were you talking to me?"

At first it didn't seem like he heard me, but then he tilted his head to the left and his eyes seemed to focus for the first time. "Who are you?" he asked.

"I'm just visiting the church." I didn't think it was wise to actually answer his question—to tell him the real reason I was there.

"How long have you been here?"

"Um . . . maybe 20 minutes. Not more."

My words didn't seem to register in a normal way. His head tilted back straight, and then he said, "How is that? How can that be true?"

I had no idea if I should continue the conversation or just walk away. Then I remembered that Phil told me to pay attention to every detail, no matter how strange or unusual. For the first time, I considered the possibility that this was more than a chance encounter, that it may have something to do with the chant. The first time I saw him was when we were sitting in the back chanting the name. Was it a coincidence, or had we somehow summoned the man? It was a thought I didn't want to explore much further.

"Do you know why I'm here?" he asked me with a voice that was filled with both anger and regret.

"I can't say I do." The words came out of my mouth almost without thinking. The fact is that I didn't know what was happening, and I wasn't sure I wanted to. "Do you know what's happening?"

He pushed the glasses over his eyes again. "Oh yes, I know what's happening. I've always known. You don't want me to leave. You come and go and think you're free, but I stay and even forget what it looks like anywhere but here. Do you have any idea how that feels? Can you imagine how hard it is to lie on this cold floor every night and then watch people walk in and out of those doors as if it's nothing?"

He looked back at the statue of St. Peter and within seconds seemed mesmerized. It was suddenly as if no one was there but him, and I wondered if there was something about the statue I was missing. I looked back hoping something would jump out at me. It was obviously an ancient sculpture, at least five feet high, and the keys he held were dramatic and almost surreal looking. And that was when I noticed where his eyes were fixed. They weren't on the statue, but something at the base of the piece, which I hadn't noticed until then. It was a Templar cross, and the man didn't seem to be able to turn away from it. He returned to the original chant: "Why am I here? Why am I here?" There was now a sorrowful sound to his voice, and I felt my heart nearly explode inside my chest.

"Can I help you?" I asked, suddenly realizing that I knew exactly what to do. He didn't seem to hear me but kept up his slow and deliberate chant. "I think I know what to do. If you can hear me, can you nod your head?"

His voice continued its unbroken mantra, but then his head began to slowly move up and down almost imperceptibly. "There's a prayer I think will help you," I said. "If you can say the words, then you may be able to leave. If that sounds like something you can do, nod your head."

Once again, the slight nod came. "Good. We're going to call on God, through the most Sacred Name. It's called the Tetragrammaton. You don't have to know what it means—just say the words with me if you can." I began to chant the name just as Phil and I had moments earlier in the back of the church but this time without substituting the name *Adonai*. I don't know why I decided to change the method Phil proposed. It felt right, though, so I decided to follow my intuition. I could see the man slowly moving his lips, first only a remote sign, then more pronounced. The energy was building inside me as we spoke the words: "*Yud Heh Vav Heh, En Sof; Yud Heh Vav Heh, En Sof; Yud Heh Vav Heh, En Sof . . .*"

His voice became loud enough for me to hear it, and I closed my eyes to focus. The energy of the name was beginning to pull me into a deep trance. All the sounds of the cathedral seemed to disappear, and I could only hear my own voice and the soft whisper of this strange man, who I wasn't even sure existed. Seconds seemed to become minutes, and as quickly as it began, I was suddenly aware of my surroundings and the sound of my voice alone. For a moment, I had the vague impression of something that reminded me of a net, or web, that spread itself throughout the basilica. I opened my eyes and realized that I was standing in front of the statue by myself. The man was gone, whoever he was, and I took a deep gulp of air.

At least two minutes passed before I was ready to move. The tours were filing past me again, and I decided to walk in the same direction, no longer against the current, until I finally found myself standing in the rear of the church where I saw Phil waiting for me. He was standing in the middle of the aisle near the back door, and he had a look on his face that made me feel he was aware that something had happened to me.

"It was the Templar cross, wasn't it?" I asked, referring to the symbol at the base of the statue. As I said those words, I looked at the exit and saw the man in black walking out through the door. His arms were open wide as if he was feeling the air for the first time.

"Yes, they're all over the place. I've been standing here for the last five minutes or so looking at them. I had the feeling it would mean something, as if it would somehow connect with whatever you were doing."

I wasn't sure if I was meant to tell him what had happened. I wasn't even sure if I believed it myself. Could it have been a figment of my imagination? For a moment, I wondered if the man I met was nothing more than a confused tourist who had wandered away from his group, and I had simply used him to fulfill some need inside me—something that would justify the stories and lessons I was learning from Phil. Maybe when I was chanting, he simply walked away and I was too deep to notice it. All these thoughts were swimming through my mind, and I didn't know what was real. I waited until we were outside before I said anything to him.

"Whatever you experienced, it wasn't your imagination," he said.

"How do you know that?"

"Because I felt it when it was happening. I knew that something was going on wherever you were. I didn't know what it was, but I knew it was something."

"Who do you think he was?"

"Who are you talking about?"

"The man. The man by the statue of Michael."

"I was looking at the statue of Michael, but I didn't see anyone."

"How is that possible? I just saw him walk out the back door a few seconds ago."

"There's no way to know for sure," Phil stated. "These are uncharted waters. It could have been an apparition, maybe even a hallucination, or perhaps it was a spirit entity that was able to actually manifest in a physical body. If I had to guess, though, I wouldn't think it was either of them."

"What was it then?"

"My guess is that it was a hyper-spatial, dimensional entity that's been trapped in the church and is occasionally able to temporarily enter into people, especially those who have a weak energy body."

"Hyper what? What does that mean?" I was really hoping that Phil was putting me on, but deep down I knew he wasn't, which really scared me.

"Just what I said—a hyper-spatial, dimensional entity. Some people, on account of a variety of health issues or various addictions, have cracks or holes that appear in their auras. It's much easier for a strong entity to enter into them and use them for a short period of time. For many, it's the only way they're able to experience the physical world for a limited time, but even so, most are somewhat confused and aren't able to interact in normal ways. Remember, these things usually happen by invitation."

"You're saying that the man I met was actually possessed by a spirit or demon?" Just saying the words made me feel strange and out of touch.

"It's certainly not possession in the way you're thinking about it. It's not like Linda Blair with heads spinning and pea soup flying around. It's actually a lot more common than you think and quite similar to the phenomenon of channeling, or transmediumship, as it used to be called. It's very much the same. More like a sharing of consciousness . . . like I said, by invitation."

"So do you think that us chanting the name drew the spirit out?"

"There's lots more to explain, Jimmy. Everything in due time. You said the first time you noticed the man was in the rear of the church when we were doing the chant, right?"

"Yes, that's correct," I affirmed, still a bit shaken.

"Then you saw him again in the back, by the statue of St. Peter. The fact that I didn't see him may mean nothing, or it may mean everything. Only time will tell. What's important is that something happened—something pretty amazing, by all accounts."

"So it was real?" I needed to hear the words out loud.

"Yes, it was real. And it's just the beginning. That was only the first name. We still have nine other places to visit." Phil began walking toward the door where the man exited moments earlier.

I thought of him with his arms outstretched feeling his freedom, perhaps for the first time. As we walked out, I felt a bit of that myself, as if my own heart was feeling free after years of constriction. All I knew for sure was that something was happening that I couldn't explain. And in that moment as we left the cathedral, I didn't want or need an explanation.

CHAPTER 7

The Marriage of
Mary Magdalene

Elohim

We walked a block to the Métro on our way to the next stop—
L'Église Sainte-Marie-Madeleine, the Church of St. Mary
Magdalene.

"Tell me what you know about this church and its history," I
said to Phil.

"It was commissioned by Napoléon Bonaparte and modeled
after the Pantheon in Rome. Napoléon's expeditions to Egypt are
the stuff of legend, but that's a story for another day. La Madeleine,
as it's called, is adorned with 52 Corinthian columns, and if you
look up, you'll notice the Ten Commandments in bas-relief on its
imposing bronze doors."

"Why the Ten Commandments?" I asked. We'd just entered the
Métro, and with our day tickets in hand, we walked through the
turnstile and then down the stairs to wait for the train.

"I really don't know, but the history isn't that important in
this case. What's significant is whom this church is dedicated to
and what it represents. There's a statue inside that I want you to
see. I'm more than curious to find out what kind of energy you feel
from it. As with Sacré-Coeur, there's a strong Templar influence at
La Madeleine, and that's one of the things we're looking for."

"Don't you mean *Magdalene*?"

"Same thing. In French, Magdalene is known as Madeleine."

"Tell me why the Templars are so important. We saw Templar crosses and other Templar imagery at Sacré-Coeur, and I sensed there were additional things as well, but I still don't understand the connection to Kabbalah or the Sacred Names."

"Following the First Crusade and the recapture of Jerusalem, the French knight Hugh de Payns, a vassal of the Count of Champagne, along with Godfrey de Saint-Omer, Andre de Montbard, and several other French knights (some say nine in all), proposed the formation of an order of monastic knights to Baldwin II, the king of Jerusalem. The function of these 'Soldiers of Christ,' or *Milice du Christ,* would be to safeguard Christian pilgrims making the very dangerous trek from the port city of Jaffa to Jerusalem. The date sometimes given for the formation of the Knights Templar is A.D. 1118, but no one knows for sure."

The train rolled into the station and we pushed our way aboard, finding a spot where we could stand together and continue our conversation. "It always struck me as strange that nine middle-aged knights would be in a position to protect Europeans making the pilgrimage to Jerusalem," I commented to Phil. "The constant threat of robbers on the road makes that seem ridiculous, not to mention the impending attack of the Saracens looking to retake the Holy Land."

"Precisely, Jimmy." I wasn't sure whether Phil was nodding in agreement or if it was from the vibration of the Métro bouncing to the next stop. "This is why it has always been held among serious researchers that the true and secret agenda of those 'Poor Fellow-Soldiers of Christ' was to have access to the Temple Mount and—"

"The Temple of Solomon, right?"

"Bingo! They spent nine years excavating the Temple Mount, and by all appearances, it would seem that they found what they were looking for . . . what they had, in fact, been sent to find."

"Who sent them?" I asked.

"The most likely candidate would have been Bernard, the abbot of Clairvaux, now known as Saint Bernard de Clairvaux. You see,

Bernard was the nephew of Andre de Montbard, who co-founded the Order along with Hugh de Payns. Pope Honorius II himself had been a member of the Cistercian Order before being elected Pope and was a close friend and confidant of Bernard.

"Obviously, Bernard had access to some very secret knowledge, mainly by virtue of his close friendship with the Pope. The Order gained official recognition and endorsement by the Roman Catholic Church in 1128 at the Council of Troyes. By 1139, with Pope Innocent II's papal bull *Omne Datum Optimum,* the Order—now known as 'The Poor Fellow-Soldiers of Christ and the Temple of Solomon' or simply 'The Order of the Temple'—was made to answer to none save the Pope himself, making them virtually untouchable and a law unto themselves."

"This is fascinating stuff, Phil, but tell me more about the excavations on the Temple Mount."

"Okay. King Baldwin of Jerusalem granted the fledgling Order quarters in a wing of the royal palace on the Temple Mount at the site of the captured Al-Aqsa Mosque, which just happens to be positioned directly above the ruins of the Temple of Solomon, the perfect location to begin their work."

I felt a wave of anticipation wash over me. "What did they find?"

"Many believe they may have found the Ark of the Covenant, which was rumored to have been buried deep underneath the Second Temple before its destruction in A.D. 70. There are clues to be found at Chartres Cathedral indicating that the Templars had actually found the Ark and carted it away. There is no doubt in my mind that the Templars found treasures, such as those described in the Copper Scroll."

"The Copper Scroll . . . I've heard of it. Wasn't it among the Dead Sea Scrolls found at Qumran?"

"Yes, in Kirbat Qumran in 1952. Written on copper, they contain lists of locations where vast treasures of gold and silver could be found. The Templars knew exactly what they were looking for and where to find it."

"When the Copper Scroll was found, did they find any treasure?"

"Only evidence of earlier excavations . . . and here's where it really gets interesting and where the connection with Kabbalah and the Sacred Names is to be found." Phil tilted his head back and brushed his hair with the fingers of both hands, like a conductor getting ready to prime his orchestra. I'd come to expect this from Phil. The only thing missing was the baton. At the same moment, though, the train made a sudden turn, nearly knocking him off balance.

"It's also rumored that the Templars found manuscripts," he said, once he repositioned himself. "These were ancient writings that had also been secreted under the Temple, deep inside Mount Moriah. I'm certain these texts covered an immense variety of subjects, ranging from architectural plans written by master masons of old to priceless books of magical knowledge dating back to earliest antiquity. Much of that knowledge came to be incorporated into what is now known as *ha-Kabbalah*. Also believed to have been found were the earliest Gospels detailing histories and accounts that could potentially shake the foundations upon which the Holy Roman Church is built . . . priceless artifacts and practical knowledge, not to mention powerful leverage that could be used against the Holy See."

"Where are these books now?" My heart was pounding in time with the rhythm of the Métro as it came halting to a stop at La Madeleine.

"I imagine that most are housed in private collections or in vaults deep within the Vatican's Secret Archives or catacombs, as well as the Smithsonian, Area 51, Wright-Patterson Air Force Base . . . places like that."

"Area 51?"

"Sure, right next to the Ark of the Covenant." He gave me a look that let me know he was kidding. At least I hoped he was.

We emerged from the Madeleine Métro station, my head spinning from Phil's tales of the Templars and hidden treasure under the Temple Mount in Jerusalem. It was just a short walk to the church. The Roman-looking exterior immediately surprised me. We headed up the steps and entered through the massive bronze doors that Phil had described, and once again I felt something expand within me as if I knew that another mystery awaited us.

Phil stopped me as we stepped inside. "Stand here for a moment and look around. Tell me if anything jumps out at you."

"What is it I'm looking for? Any hints at all?"

"You'll know it when you see it," he answered.

As I looked around, my attention was immediately drawn to the main altar of the church, which is dominated by a wondrous and massive statue of Mary Magdalene being held aloft and carried to Heaven. The *Ascension of Mary Magdalene* is an incredible piece of art, but nothing immediately seemed out of place. I looked around more, amazed by the sheer scale and beauty of the statue and the surrounding layout of the church, but once again nothing happened. As I started moving closer to the statue, however, something else drew my attention. I looked to my right, toward the very rear of the church, and I saw what Phil meant. There was a side altar with a very large statue of three people: Jesus, Mary Magdalene, and another man who looked like John the Baptist. The scene seemed to be a blessing or even a marriage, with John the Baptist standing over Jesus and Mary Magdalene, who were kneeling and holding hands.

"Ah, you found it," Phil said.

"What is it I found?"

"What do you think is happening here?" Phil was pointing at the statue.

"Actually, it looks very much like John the Baptist is marrying them. It's hard to mistake the image."

"That's what seems to be happening, doesn't it?" Phil had that typically ironic look that made me think he wasn't telling me something. "That's one of the things that makes this church so unique. Legends of Mary and Jesus's marriage are very popular here in France, especially in the south. It's more than mere speculation at this point that the Magdalene came here after the Resurrection and spent her last years in Provence. Mary Magdalene is venerated in France like no other place, except perhaps in Wales or the Dalmatian region of Croatia. There's certainly a degree of corroborative evidence that supports the idea that Jesus and Mary were married, and that some time after the crucifixion, Mary carried their daughter to France. These are teachings that have been obscured by the church, but that doesn't alter the fact that it has been believed here for nearly 2,000 years."

"So why would the church allow a statue like this to remain?" I asked. "Why wouldn't they just have it removed?"

"I have my ideas. The church is certainly privy to more knowledge than they let on. Maybe they're afraid of the outcry if they removed it, or maybe they like it exactly where it is. All I know is that it's here, and it speaks volumes."

"Do you think the statue has anything to do with the reason we're here?"

"You mean energies or entities being held hostage?"

"That's a nice way of putting it," I remarked. "I would have said something about devils and such."

"I know you would. That's because you still don't really know what we're up to. Anyway, to answer your question, I'm not at all sure. I also don't want to get in the way of you sensing things yourself. I'd hate to complicate matters with all my opinions. Why don't we get right to work and look at the next Sacred Name?"

We sat down in the back away from the other people. There were far less people there than at the Basilica of the Sacred Heart, but we still couldn't afford to look too conspicuous. Phil opened his notepad and closed his eyes. "First of all, I want to begin with a prayer that invokes the energy of what's known in Jewish mysticism as the *Shekinah,* which is the feminine aspect of the Godhead. Remember, this church is dedicated to one of the greatest women adepts in history, so it feels appropriate."

"Tell me more about the Shekinah."

"Well, it originally referred to the Divine Presence, the presence of God in this world. In Kabbalah, the Shekinah was given what's known as a 'mythic independence'—in other words, it's considered to be an aspect of God that's in a state of exile from God, from itself.

You see, with the exile of the Jewish people after the destruction of the Second Temple in A.D. 70, it has been said that the Shekinah was with them, accompanying them in their exile. At the End of Days, when God's Holy Sparks—"

"God's Holy Sparks?" I interrupted.

"Yes, the children, or 'ecclesia of Israel.' When the children of Israel have been liberated, and that can be taken in a variety of ways, it is believed that the Messiah will come and the Temple will be restored. When this happens, God's bride, the Shekinah, will come out of exile, and the Temple will be rebuilt for her. It's all about the mystical union. You see, the good deeds we do in this world, called *mitzvoth,* are for the sake of the reunion of God and his bride, according to tradition.

"When we've reconciled our dual natures and reintegrated the male and female within—when the Bride is reunited with the Beloved—then we will see her in her white radiance, and we'll get to play in fields of holy apple trees, upon whose branches beautiful blue apples grow . . . or so they say. She is the name of the rose, a lily among thorns and the dove of peace. At the time of Tikkun, the time of redemption, God will be reunited with his lost bride. In myth and fairy tale, she is the lost princess, the imprisoned princess, the exiled bride, the lost bride. She is also known as the Queen of the Sabbath. She is the beautiful virgin who has no eyes."

"Why is she blind?"

"She lost her eyes from weeping in her exile. In this state of cosmic exile, she wears black, with no light of her own, and like the moon she reflects only the light of the sun. She is the Virgin of the Torah, upon whom no eyes are directed. It is said the *created* Torah is the outer garment of the Shekinah, the Torah as it was revealed to the world of men."

"That's really amazing."

"Why is it amazing?"

"I can't believe how easily you remember all that. It flows out of your mouth like you're reading it from a book."

"When you're passionate about something, it's easy to remember every detail," he added. "I'm sure you, of all people, know what I mean. There have been times when I've heard you speak in seminars or retreats when you tap into that flow, and everyone in the room is transported to what I like to call the 'Land of Faerie,' the place that is 'within and beyond all things,' to borrow a phrase from Joseph Campbell."

"Wasn't it the poet Kabir who said, 'Bring the vision of the Beloved into your heart'?"

"It was. So in honor of all the great romantic poets, all seekers of love, wisdom, and truth, let's go ahead and say a prayer to her." Phil bowed his head and crossed his hands over his heart. I did the same. "Here at L'Église Sainte-Marie-Madeleine, built in memory of Her—the Divine Sophia, the Divine Wisdom in the person of Mary Magdalene—at the time of the Restoration, when the Temple, the Temple in Man, will be restored . . . our bodies becoming chariots for the Shekinah, we open and offer ourselves in service. We ask that the indwelling presence of God be reunited with his lost bride who will liberate us from our bondage in the lower worlds. Amen, and so it is."

As we prayed, I felt myself being filled with a strange emotion— doubt. I wasn't aware of anything that triggered the filling, but it seemed to be growing. I decided to simply stay with it and see where it would lead.

When Phil finished the prayer, he looked over at me. "Now that we've prayed to the Divine Sophia, we can begin." He took a deep breath. "The name we're going to use now is *Elohim*, which is the third word in the Hebrew book of Genesis, and its common translation is simply 'God'—God in its creative aspect. It's associated with *Hod*, the eighth sphere on the Tree of Life, connecting it with wisdom and splendor. It's important to acknowledge that this name, like all the others, has multiple levels or layers of meaning. For the time being and for our purposes here, though, I'd like for us to understand *Elohim* as it corresponds to the 'penetration of wisdom' and as an element of a geometrical process that brought the world into being."

He then closed his notebook and set it down on the pew. "Now we're going to chant the name 12 times, and we'll add the *En Sof* at the end like we did before. Are you ready?"

"Yes, I am."

"Okay, let's begin."

I closed my eyes and took a deep breath. Then we started: "*Elohim, En Sof; Elohim, En Sof; Elohim, En Sof . . .*"

I counted each time on my hand the way that Phil had shown me. When we finished, we sat in silence for a while until I heard Phil shift in the pew. "Let's open up and see what happens," he said. "Go ahead and wander about. If you need me, I'll be here in the back."

I stood up and slowly began walking toward the front of the church. The sound of a woman singing Vivaldi drifted through the speakers, a recording they must have decided added to the sacredness of the experience. I preferred silence to the music and decided to focus on the pictures and other statues, as I looked for clues or any other sensations that arose. The feeling of doubt had grown stronger since beginning the chant. It was almost too much to bear, and I wondered what was causing this sudden internal shift. There was no thought or situation that came to mind that could explain it, and I had no other choice but to consider that it was inspired by whatever energy, or entity, we had come to visit and to hopefully aid in its release.

I was nearly in front of the altar. A rope was looped lazily through holes in the walls to keep tourists away from the tabernacle, so I stood just beyond looking at the statue of Mary Magdalene being carried to Heaven. On her face was a look of profound ecstasy, as if she wasn't even aware that she was being lifted. As if in contrast to what Mary must have been feeling, I felt as if I was being pushed down, not lifted up. The heaviness in my heart was beginning to spread to the rest of my body. There seemed to be a tangible force adding weight to my emotions, but I could neither explain nor directly perceive it. The more I looked at the statue, the more pronounced the feeling became until I wasn't sure what I would do. Part of me wanted to run out of the church and perhaps not stop until I was out of Paris—away from Phil and everything he was trying to convince me of. At the same time, however, it was the moment in which I was most convinced of the importance of being there. The emotion that was building inside me wasn't self-created—I was sure of it—but was being required of me somehow, and no explanation seemed more tangible than the unseen forces we were seeking.

I looked above the altar to a perfectly lit painting depicting a long procession of saints just above the statue of Mary Magdalene. They all looked toward the central figure of Jesus with arms outstretched in blessing. Some seemed to be filled with awe and wonder while others stood as if unaware of their surroundings. I looked from one to the other wondering who they were or what they represented. One saint, several people to the left of Jesus, held a staff in both hands and seemed focused on the heavenly scene. When my eyes rested on this figure, the heaviness I felt seemed to increase, and when I looked away from him in either direction, it began to dissipate. I tested this several times until I realized that the energy, or the feeling, was actually radiating from this one figure. Whatever it was I experienced, it started there.

I walked away from the altar hoping I was wrong. How was it possible that a painting could radiate an emotion and it would have an effect on people as they gazed at it? When I reached the very rear of the church, the feeling felt like a drum pounding inside my chest. There seemed to be a band of energy, almost like a giant rubber band, pulling me back to the altar, back to the painting and the saint with his staff. I turned around and walked as fast as I could without being obvious. When I arrived at the spot where I stood a moment earlier, I almost expected the picture to have changed, for the staff to have shifted in his hands or for him to be facing the other direction. It hadn't changed, but the feeling when I stared up at it hadn't changed either, and I looked around hoping to find Phil standing nearby.

When I realized I was alone, I felt an immediate sense of relief. As much as I wanted Phil to tell me what he thought or what to do, I knew this was something I had to discover on my own. I closed my eyes and took a deep breath, then squinted as I looked again. For the first time, I thought I recognized something different about this particular saint, as if there was a faint glow around his body. I closed my eyes and looked again. Now it was even more pronounced, and I also felt something stirring inside me, something different from the emotion I'd been feeling since beginning the prayer . . . more of a voice or thought that seemed to be forming inside my mind. I tried to clear away all other thoughts so I could discern what I felt or heard. Within seconds, words seemed to form, only four, but I was almost sure that they were not from my own mind.

"Stop what you're doing."

Was I simply getting to the point where I was imagining demons everywhere I looked, or were the words actually coming from the man in the picture? And how could a painting be alive and speak to another person who happens to pass beneath its gaze? The whole idea seemed ludicrous, yet I couldn't deny what I was sensing. I decided to answer the words, to see if I could actually enter into a conversation. Maybe if I could hear more, then I would know what this was and why it was happening.

"Stop what you're doing," the man in the painting seemed to say again.

"I'm not sure what you mean," I answered. "What do you want me to stop?"

"Stop what you're doing."

"Please speak to me . . . tell me more. Why are you here?"

There was a long pause, and for a moment I thought the communication had stopped. Then more words came. *"Let me be. Why are you doing this? Go away. Leave me alone!"*

When he said those words, the doubt I felt turned to anger. It filled me like fire, and I wanted to explode. Although I knew the feeling wasn't my own, it felt like it came from the very core of my being, and I used all my strength to push it away. The faint glow around the picture was now a bright pink, and I was forced to sit down in a chair that stood against the wall. As I did, I felt the sensation lessen but only enough for me to compose my thoughts and speak again. "Please," I responded. "I'm not here to hurt you. I'm here to help."

"I do not need your help."

"I came here to pray."

"You came to displace me."

"I mean you no harm. I came to invoke an aspect of the God-force within me, in the name of *Elohim*. I'm here to bless you . . . not to curse you."

All the emotions seemed to drain from my body as I spoke. I was engulfed by a profound silence, and it was a welcomed relief. I stood up again and walked over to the rope and then looked directly up at the man in the painting. "I don't know how long you've been here," I said, almost aloud, "but you don't have to stay. We've brought the name here to help release you from your bondage and guide you home."

No answer. I continued, "I'm sure you don't want to stay here forever. Whoever you are and wherever you belong, I'm sure you'll be much happier."

No answer. "Please, you must understand that I am only here to be of service. I want you to be free so you can be happy again."

The voice suddenly returned. *"Free?"* he added, in a low, almost reverential, tone.

What felt like a gentle wind seemed to brush against my face, and I stepped back from it in amazement. The feelings of doubt and anger were gone, and I knew I was alone. I turned around and looked toward the back of the church. That was when I saw Phil. He was standing with his arms at his side, gesturing with a tilt of his head toward the spot where I'd felt the presence. His eyes were closed, and I wondered how long he had been standing there. When I felt I was able, I began walking toward him.

"Did you feel any of that?" I asked.

"I felt all of it, although I'm not exactly sure what happened."

That was when I looked down and saw where he was standing. There was a very large Templar cross on the floor, with Phil in the very center. "A Templar cross," I remarked. "That has some significance to what just happened, doesn't it?"

"I think it might be better if we left now," he said. "Whatever it was we came to do, it's over now. We can discuss everything as we walk."

As we stepped out of the church, I realized that the energy and emotion I felt had completely vanished. The cool wet air felt amazing against my face, and I pulled the collar of my coat around my neck to avoid the chill. We walked down the stone steps until we were once again on the sidewalk, and then we crossed the street and turned left. I explained what I'd experienced with the painting and the energy I felt. "Is it possible that some kind of, how do you call it, interdimensional entity, could attach itself to a painting like that . . . then react when it felt us there?"

"I love it when you say words like *interdimensional entity*," Phil commented, smiling. "But, seriously, I think you already know the answer to that question. It's possible because it just happened to you, didn't it? Imagine that it was a painting of you. Imagine that somehow you've been drawn there and regardless of the reason, you believe that you can't leave. You're imprisoned. You look around trying to find something you can identify with, something that feels familiar. Then you notice a painting that either reminds you of yourself or perhaps you want or need to insinuate yourself into the scene portrayed in it for whatever reason. In this regard, you literally inhabit the painting. Does that make sense? Think of the painting again and the emotion you felt when you looked at it. What did you say it was?"

"It was doubt, then a heaviness in my heart and the feeling that I was weighed down."

Phil put a hand on my shoulder. I noticed we were walking down a street called Saint Honoré. Just at that moment, a balloon freed itself from the hand of a small child walking between his parents. As they passed us the boy stared at me, seemingly oblivious to the fact that his balloon was ascending over the streets and boulevards of Paris. It was a strange moment given the subject we were discussing, and I wondered if there was some kind of correlation.

"So whoever or whatever it was, it identified itself so completely with the figure in the painting that it actually thought it was the image?" I asked. "That's a bit like what we all do—identify with an image or a projection of ourselves rather than the truth. You can call it the ego or whatever, but in the end, it's the exact same thing."

"I think you're beginning to understand, Jimmy. One of the most beautiful of the Gnostic Gospels is the 'Hymn of the Pearl.' It talks about the merging or the union of the image and the angel—that the Prince of Peace sees in the Angel of Light his true reflection, that there's an image of ourselves preserved for us in the higher Heavens. It's written that name and image become one, see? When we can elevate and exalt our thoughts to having no thought devoid of a consciousness of ourselves as Divine Creations, then we'll be able to reclaim the 'garment of light' we lost at the time of the Fall. The names we're using are surely exalted thoughts. I believe you may have given this fallen angel an image of itself it hasn't seen for a very long time."

I thought of the boy and his balloon. Was it possible that some form of sentient intelligence or confused spirit was now free and soaring over the streets of Paris toward Heaven? The thought brought me a feeling of solace. Then I turned back to Phil, saying, "That's amazing, but how did it make me feel those emotions—the doubt and the anger?"

"We feel what we feel, Jimmy. You helped me learn that lesson . . . that in the end, we are responsible only to ourselves for what we feel and what we create."

As he said those words, combined with the light rain that was falling, I felt a sense of clarity and purpose that I couldn't quite grasp . . . but it felt wonderful.

"I think that it was its only defense." Phil continued, "A skill mastered over hundreds and hundreds of years. Who knows how may others have had a similar experience but didn't have the knowledge base to understand it. They probably felt the same things you felt. Maybe it stimulated the memory of some troubling event in their life or in a past life. When they felt those same feelings, it made them leave. The difference here is that we didn't leave. We decided to stay and help."

"One last question," I added. "When I saw you standing on the Templar cross, it seemed like you were helping me somehow."

"I was," he replied. "I saw you there and realized you were in some kind of distress. It was pretty obvious. I noticed the cross on the floor and knew that by standing on it and using a few choice words, I could project some energy to you. Do you remember what I said about these symbols being like batteries that keep things charged? As far as I can tell, it helped you get over the hump. That's when you seemed to regain your strength."

"That's two entities in so many churches. It makes me wonder what we're in store for next."

"Well, you won't have to wonder long," he said as he stopped in the sidewalk. "We're on our way to the next location."

CHAPTER 8

The Nun and the Icon

Yah

The Church of Our Lady of the Assumption . . . we would have walked by it if Phil hadn't abruptly stopped on the sidewalk. We turned to the right and walked up several stairs until we were inside. It was small compared to the first two places we visited, but as with most churches in Europe, it was just as much a marvel. We stood in the back for a moment and looked around. The altar was dominated by a painting of the Blessed Mother praying, or listening, to an angel that hovered slightly above her. To the left of the altar hung an ancient-looking icon of Mother Mary wearing a crown of 12 stars and standing on a crescent moon, her hands folded over her chest. Gold leaves covered most areas, giving the church a sacred glow, and the smell of incense filled the air.

"What do you know about this church?" I whispered to Phil.

"To be honest, this wasn't the one I had originally intended for us to go to. I just stopped here for directions or maybe for *direction*, as it turns out. We'll make it to Saint-Roch sooner or later, but now that we're here, I'm feeling a sensation I can't deny. I think we're meant to be here . . . as if we don't have a choice."

"I thought you had a total of ten locations you planned for us to visit. Won't this throw us off by one if we stay?"

"Actually, I figured something like this into the equation. I sensed that Spirit might take us off the grid, so to speak, so I factored this eventuality in." Then he paused. "I can already tell why."

"What do you mean?"

"I'm not going to say anything for now. I'd like to see if you can notice it on your own. All I'll say is there's something here that is quite extraordinary given the *raison d'être* for this tour, as it were. Remember that we're here to draw upon the grace and power found within the many names of God to help release blocked energies within ourselves that will in turn help release certain forms of sentient consciousness that may be imprisoned within these sacred places. That being said, there's something important that you should be able to pick out rather easily."

I looked around again. "Really . . . I don't see anything that strikes me as strange."

"Look again."

I carefully gazed around the church, trying to pick out any detail that seemed out of place or that could be connected with our mission. I didn't see anything except exquisite pieces of art and then . . . "Wait! Above the altar, just over the painting of Mary and the angel—there's a golden pyramid with rays shooting out from it. Aren't those Hebrew letters inside the pyramid? Isn't that the Tetragrammaton, the name we used at Sacred Heart?"

"Very good!" Phil affirmed. "The Highest Name of God in this church, right above the altar—that can't be a coincidence."

"But what does it mean? If the name is enthroned right here on the altar, then how could the energy get trapped?"

"There are many possibilities. Remember, I told you that many of these churches were built with the added purpose of restraining or containing certain energies that were never meant to wander the earth until such time as various celestial alignments occurred. Then they could be guided back to where they belong. Another reason may be that the force of the name itself could have pulled something in. We have to be open to all of the possibilities. Let's sit down and do our chant and see what we discover."

When we first entered the church, there was a lone woman in her late 20s sitting in the front pew. She seemed to be deep in prayer, periodically looking up at the painting of Mary and the angel, and then raising her head slightly to settle her gaze on the Tetragrammaton . . . or so it seemed. As impatient as I was to begin, there was something about this girl in the act of prayer that gave me pause. By the time she finished, stood up, crossed herself, and slowly walked out, a few other people had filed in. Not even a minute passed before they left as well, and we were alone.

"What is the name we'll be using?" I inquired.

"The Sacred Name we'll be chanting here is *Yah*. It's generally thought that this word is a shortened form of YHWH, the four-lettered name of God. Moses Maimonides considered it, along with *Ehyeh Asher Ehyeh*, to be the true explanation of the *Shem ha-Meforesh*, the Tetragrammaton. He defined it as 'everlasting life' or alternatively, 'He or She Is.' This name of God occurs about 50 times in the Tanakh."

"The Tanakh?"

"The Bible of Judaism. The name *Yah* is also found in 'hallelu-*yah*,' meaning 'praise the Lord.'"

"The fact that it's short for YHWH should be significant, don't you think?"

"Yah man, it just might be," Phil quipped in a Jamaican accent. "The other thing to remember is that the first letter of the Tetragrammaton is the Yud, and it's connected with Yah, through the sphere of Chokmah on the Tree of Life. It's funny how things keep coming back to your comma."

"And in this depiction, it's above the other letters."

"Yes, as you said, it's the letter of transcendence. The Talmud states that God used the letter *Heh* to create the world but will use the Yud to create the world to come. It's all coming together so perfectly. Let's go ahead and chant the name 12 times and see what happens."

We both took a deep breath. I held out my left hand and Phil his right in order to begin counting. "Remember to pay close attention while we're chanting," Phil said. "There may be powerful forces released here that manifest in some fashion. Just be aware of everything—your feelings, even the temperature in the room. Nothing is insignificant." We took another deep breath, and he continued. "It's nice to be the only ones here. Let's begin with a prayer: We'll be using the Holy Name *Yah* in this Temple of Divine Science. The name is one of the *Shemot ha-Elohim,* the pillar names of God, and corresponds to the sphere of Chokmah on the Tree of Life. The sphere of Chokmah, which corresponds to wisdom, is the sphere through which the light of the *En Sof* illuminates the 'world of emanation.' The light that emerges through the sphere is just as pure as the light that entered it, making this the actual Light of Divinity."

I leaned in closer to Phil. "That all sounded great, but do you realize that I didn't understand a single word?"

"Ne vous inquiétez pas, mon ami," he replied coyly. "You don't have to understand the words if you can hear the music they make." He smiled and put down the notebook he'd been reading from. He glanced over to the high altar. I could just make out the reflection of the Tetragrammaton with its golden rays in Phil's eyes before he closed them. "Let's repeat the name 12 times."

And we began: *"Yah, En Sof; Yah, En Sof; Yah, En Sof . . ."*

As before, the chant seemed to delve deep to the core of my being. Phil always stressed that we weren't there to release the energy of spirits that were somehow outside or separate from us, but that we were there to let the Sacred Names release energy blocked in our own hearts. He also said that using the names would help open gates within us, giving us access to vast storehouses of knowledge, as well as allowing grace to come into and through us into the world. I remembered him saying something about space and time overlapping or that many different dimensions were blending—information that was usually over my head . . . over most people's heads, I imagined.

I'm not sure what made this come to my mind at that particular moment, but I couldn't seem to shake it. According to Phil, the gates that would open in us when we chanted the various names would correspond to the portals or stargates through which certain entities could pass through to find their way home and continue the reeducation of their souls. Once released, then a resonant vibration would help the same energy release everything around it. That, as I understood it, was the reason why we were there.

Each of the places Phil chose—or that chose him . . . I really wasn't sure which at this point—seemed to host some form of trapped consciousness, a spirit or entity, a light or dark angel. Perhaps it was even a demon that had either been drawn there intentionally or one that, as Phil might say, got caught in the cross fire. Once we embodied each of the names, these entities would somehow present themselves to us and then have the opportunity to be released. I was skeptical at first, but after two such experiences, my doubts were quickly fading.

My eyes were closed as we finished the chant. I opened them to see that Phil had already walked away from the pew, and I thought it was strange that I didn't hear him leave. Had I gone that deep? And how much time had passed? Phil was on the far side of the church looking at the icon of Mary to the left of the main altar. I stood up and felt my knees wobble a bit before I found my balance. Then I stepped out and noticed myself instinctively walking toward the altar, to the Tetragrammaton.

Golden rays of light radiated outward from the pyramid with the Holy Name. I noticed the Yud, the first letter that began on the right side of the word and was suspended above the rest. I listened within to see if there was anything I could discern or hear. Nothing came to me. My instinct told me that I was on the right track, although I still hadn't been able to identify anything in particular.

I looked at the Tetragrammaton again. There was something significant about it—I was sure—but there didn't seem to be anything unusual to lead me in one direction or the other. I thought about the Yud and everything it represents. It's the "hand of God" and symbolizes Divine Inspiration coming into form. I thought that the bottom of the letter, the tail, might be pointing in a particular direction. I'm not sure what made me think this, but it entered my mind as if it came from somewhere outside of my consciousness. I tried to follow the trail to see what it pointed to. It shot away from the center of the altar toward the left, apparently to the floor just between the altar and the icon of Mary. I decided to stand on that spot and see if I felt anything unusual. The air seemed to be colder in a very small area just in front of the icon. I stepped away, then stepped back. Yes, it was definitely colder there, but what that meant, I still wasn't sure.

I moved to the pew directly across from the cold spot. Phil had moved away from the icon and was moving from one side of the church to the other, so I decided not to ask for his help. Just as before, I felt that this was something I'd have to figure out on my own, as much as I would have loved an ally. I sat staring at the spot hoping something would happen. At least two minutes went by, and I was almost ready to search for another plan.

That's when I felt something move—not so much from the outside but from within me. It felt as if my stomach jerked forward, but it was accompanied by a sensation of profound devotion. My heart filled with intense joy and an unbelievable sense of love. I stood up and walked over to the spot I'd found. It was still cold, but the wonderful sensation seemed to increase as I stood there. I almost didn't want to leave, but I then felt that I was intruding on something or someone, although I had no idea what that meant. I went back to the pew and knelt down. I closed my eyes and began to pray, which seemed like the only appropriate measure given the supreme sensation I was still experiencing. My heart was expanding and filling with light. I tried to focus on the feeling and for a moment the urgency of discovering the cause vanished. All I wanted to do was bask in the beauty of the sensation, and to feel such an intimate, holy connection with God.

Then I felt an image forming in my mind. At first it seemed like a mist or a ghostly figure, but within seconds, it gained solid form and I could make out the figure of a nun kneeling on the cold stone floor in front of the icon. She wore an ancient habit, the kind I often saw in old paintings, which hadn't been worn by most orders for at least a hundred years. Her back was turned to me in the vision, so I couldn't see her face, but the feeling of love continued to increase.

Then a new thought came to me. If I was actually perceiving the spirit of a nun who was trapped there, maybe I should leave her alone. This was not at all like the other two situations, where the spirits were antagonistic and gave me an uncomfortable feeling. Who was this nun hurting? If anything, she was lost in a rapturous experience that most people would give anything to achieve. She was in Heaven, not hell, and I considered whether it would be better to let her be.

But she wasn't in Heaven, and I knew it. For whatever reason, she was caught between Heaven and Earth and probably didn't realize that she was there at all. She thought she was in the convent praying and that her devotion had brought her to the highest and most coveted of spiritual experiences—perfect union. But the fact of the matter was that she was trapped in the church, and she wouldn't be free until she was released. Then her meditation would be complete, and she would be able to worship God face-to-face, not from this unbearable distance. Once again, I thought about calling Phil, but the moment was so tender and sublime I decided to hold the energy on my own.

But what was I meant to do? The thought of chanting the name again entered my mind. At the very least, it could give me some kind of inspiration—something that might lead me to being of some help or benefit. I closed my eyes again and began repeating the Holy Name: "*Yah, En Sof; Yah, En Sof; Yah, En Sof . . .*"

In my vision, the nun seemed to hear my words and slowly turned her head in my direction, searching for the source of the chant. Her skin was as white as snow, and she didn't seem to be more than 30 years old. She was beautiful, and I almost lost my concentration looking at her. I decided to add a message to the chant since this seemed to be the only way she could hear my voice. At the same time, I felt as if I were enmeshed in some kind of web or net of light. I'm not sure how I did this, but I encoded an intention onto the words, which was simply, *The Mother is calling you home. The Mother is calling you home. . . .*

Her eyes twitched, and I wondered if she'd heard me. A look of confusion seemed to fill her face, and she looked down at her hands as if she were waking from a dream. Then she gazed at the icon again, and I could feel her confusion vanish. I suddenly sensed that she was floating toward the icon of Mary. Her hands were now open wide as if she were about to embrace the Mother. Then she disappeared, and I realized I was alone.

I opened my eyes again and looked around. Phil was still on the other side of the church, but he was now looking in my direction. We were alone again, especially now that the ecstatic nun had passed beyond my ability to perceive her.

"Is everything okay?" he asked.

I took a deep breath. "Yes, everything is great . . . even more than I can say."

✧✧✧✧✧

CHAPTER 9

Saint-Roch and the Cross Pattée

Shaddai el Chai

We left the church but paused on the steps. "Something happened, didn't it?" Phil inquired.

I told him everything I experienced, and he listened intently. I talked about following the Yud, feeling that it would lead me in the right direction. Then I noticed the cold spot in front of the icon, ultimately sensing the presence of the beautiful nun. Finally, I explained how chanting the name *Yah* seemed to awaken her, as if she had fallen into a deep prayerful trance. Once awakened, she was able to see the icon as a portal—her gate or path to freedom. She then vanished, merging with the icon she so adored.

Phil smiled. "That's really amazing. An interesting detour, as it were, if in fact it was a detour. Very different from the other two, wouldn't you agree?"

"Thankfully," I answered. "After the ghost in the painting, I was ready for the nun." We turned onto St. Honoré and began to walk. Phil's pace was brisk. I could see he was in a hurry to get to our next destination. "Where are we off to now?" I asked, doing my best to keep up.

"We're going to a church dedicated to a 13th-century saint named Saint Roch. It's just up the street here on the left."

"I've never heard of him."

"Very interesting person, as you'll see. From the moment he was born, he was a miracle. His mother was unable to conceive, so when her son came into the world, everyone thought it was an act of God. This was supported by the fact that he had a birthmark on his chest, a small red cross that grew as he grew. He was known for it. His family was very affluent in Montpellier, and both his parents died when he was 20. He was meant to be governor of the area and to wield great influence over the region, but he instead decided to follow the example of St. Francis of Assisi. He gave everything to the poor and went to Rome. When he arrived, the city was in the midst of a great plague, and Roch became known as a healer. Whenever he would make the sign of the cross on individuals, they would live. A little later, he became ill and was expelled from the city. The only way he survived was by training a local dog to bring him bread to a little hut he'd built. Fascinating story, don't you think?"

"Does it have some relevance to what we're doing here?"

"That's what we're here to find out. I'm intrigued by the cross on his body—a red cross, no less, like the Templars—and also how he would heal people. So far, all the places we've visited today had something in common: there was significant Templar influence in the architecture or in concrete symbols, such as the Templar cross, the cross pattée. In the case of the Church of the Assumption, we were guided by the four-lettered name of God, the Tetragrammaton. There seems to be a theme developing here that's informing our Parisian adventure, wouldn't you agree? I suggest we continue to pay very close attention to any and all signs and synchronies, letting them continue to guide us."

"Tell me more about the significance of the Templar cross."

"Well, where did we leave off? I don't know if you know this—actually, I don't know if many people know this—but the cross first used by the Templars was called the Cross of Lorraine. In 1146, at the behest of our old friend St. Bernard of Clairvaux, Pope Eugenius III substituted the now iconic red cross that we're familiar with in place of the Cross of Lorraine. This was done purportedly as a symbol of martyrdom, according to the 13th-century bishop of

Acre, Jacques de Vitry. I think that was his name. Anyway, the red color of the cross may represent the blood of Christ."

"Or maybe his bloodline." I added, as if the thought appeared in my mind without my being consciously aware of its origin.

"That may very well be, Jimmy. The color red is often associated with Mary Magdalene. There are, however, more esoteric associations with the Templar cross. Would you like to hear the one that has the most relevance in terms of what we're doing here?"

"I'm all ears." As the words left my mouth, the sky opened up, and instead of the light misty drizzle that had been falling since we began our quest, it started to rain harder.

"The great storm!" he shouted, covering the backpack that contained his notepad. "Yahweh must have been listening in and wants us to continue inside." We ran for cover toward the entrance to the Church of Saint-Roch.

We stepped into the massive church, the largest from the Baroque period. According to Phil, the foundation was built in 1653 and was one of the most important churches in Paris. It was awe inspiring, and some of the most magnificent paintings and sculptures I had ever seen filled each corner and wall. The ceiling in particular was a masterpiece. The domed roof portrayed biblical scenes, including Jesus with his hand outstretched in blessing. It was difficult to imagine that such a place could also host energies that remained unseen by human eyes.

"It's crucial to understand," Phil stated, "and I think you already know or at least suspect that these churches and cathedrals are built on the sites of earlier churches, temples, or structures that performed much the same functions—"

"Like holding these energies?" I interrupted.

"Yes, I would agree. Many of these energies have been around a long time, long before we appeared on the scene. I'm talking a *looong* time." He extended the word to add emphasis.

"How do you suggest we begin?"

"If you look around, you'll see some of the most amazing art and architecture. The Main Lady Chapel houses a collection of religious art that is virtually unparalleled in all of Paris. Saint-Roch was designed by the same architect who designed the Louvre, and it contains something very special, which you'll discover in due time." He motioned for me to follow him to a pew in the back. "The name we're going to use here is *Shaddai el Chai* or *El Shaddai*. Among its many meanings are the 'Lord God Almighty,' 'Almighty God Lives Forever,' 'Almighty Living Creature of God,' and 'God Almighty Who Is Sufficient.' In Exodus 6:3, Yahweh is identified with El Shaddai, as he was known to the Patriarchs. *Shaddai* itself is one of ten Divine Names quoted in the rabbinic legend of the angelic hierarchies. It's the Divine Name for the Sphere of Yesod on the Tree of Life. Its name can be used for protection and, perhaps more important, it can be used to summon jinni."

"You mean *jinni* as in *genie*?" I was beginning to feel yet another piece fall into place.

"Absolutely. Do you think that all the genies loosened upon this world since the beginning of time are all bottled up safe and sound? Guess again. Think about it . . . it's very interesting considering what we're up to, don't you think?"

Unlike our last experience, Saint-Roch had many visitors—most, it seemed, were just trying to get out of the rain. I wondered if we'd be able to keep a low profile. We sat down, Phil unzipped his pack, and then he opened up his notebook. "I can only hope that our experience with the beautiful nun marks a definite turn for us," I remarked.

"I wouldn't get too comfortable in that idea," Phil answered, his voice taking on a decidedly ominous tone. "I'm already getting the feeling that this is going to be different."

His words shot through me like poisonous darts. I was hoping we would confront more angels than demons in our quest, but when I closed my eyes and took a deep breath—allowing myself to feel deep into the cavernous church where we sat—I realized that I also sensed it. There seemed to be a confused energy enveloping the entire area. And just like the previous experiences, it was beginning to work its way into my emotional body. I took a deep breath and opened my eyes again, and then I noticed that Phil was sitting with his head bowed.

"Are you okay?"

"Yes, I'll be fine. I'm just getting ready."

"Getting ready for what?" He didn't answer me, which made me even more nervous. Whatever was about to happen, it was something we would need all our energy for.

"As I mentioned," Phil said as he sat up, "the name we're going to call upon is *Shaddai el Chai.* El Shaddai is also known as the 'God of the Mountain.' Please understand that when we call upon these Divine expressions, we're tapping into archetypal, primeval forces that were worshipped long before the creation of the world, not to mention *ha-Kabbalah.* This is not the mere evoking of lesser Gods, as many would believe. Those who think this are as guilty as those who see only the outer garment of all the works of higher calling. These names represent nothing less than the elements of creation. We know that we're here to do good work, and that there are many powerful allies on our side. After a short prayer of protection, we'll repeat the name 12 times, ending each with *En Sof.*"

Phil said the prayer and then bowed his head. We repeated the chant together: *"Shaddai el Chai, En Sof; Shaddai el Chai, En Sof; Shaddai el Chai, En Sof . . ."*

Our lowered voices echoed off the stone walls just to our right, and I could feel myself becoming more confused as we chanted. I could neither explain nor truly identify this energy, and when I looked over at Phil, he seemed to be having a similar experience. His eyes were closed, and his mouth was tight as he recited the words. I wondered if we had simply talked ourselves into the feelings of anxiety and foreboding, but the longer it persisted, the more I realized we weren't making it up. Something was happening, but it was still unclear what it was.

When we finished, Phil and I sat still for a moment, contemplating what our next move was. He was the first one to stir. "So let's walk around and see what happens."

"Just don't wander too far away," I replied as I stood up. "I want you to be near me if anything goes wrong."

"You don't have to worry. Nothing too far out of the ordinary will happen here."

His words didn't seem to match the look in his eyes. I knew he was as concerned as I was, although I didn't know why. The feeling of confusion had now increased to the point that I wasn't sure what to do. I didn't know if I should walk toward the altar or stay in the rear of the church. I looked back to the ceiling and hoped to find some inspiration. The saints and apostles there were silent. I finally decided not to think at all but to follow my instincts. It said to go to the altar, and so I did.

I passed many side altars on the way to the front, and my steps felt slow and uncommitted. When I finally arrived, I stood looking at the tabernacle, wondering if the source of the energy I was feeling emanated from there. I somehow knew that it wasn't. I felt drawn to the rear, just behind the main altar. I began walking and noticed that my steps had a stronger purpose than before. The first thing I noticed was a replica of the Ark of the Covenant, the legendary casing that once held the Ten Commandments. Phil was already standing there, so I walked over to him.

"That's pretty amazing," I commented.

"The Ark of the Covenant, or the Ark of the Testimony, which is a more accurate description. A pretty good replica, if memory serves. Why do you think it's here?"

"Me? I'm not sure, but the energy I've been feeling seems to be coming from somewhere in this area, maybe this very spot."

"What do you know about the Ark?" Phil asked. Smiling, he continued, "Aside from the Indiana Jones version, which, to be honest, wasn't too far off the mark." He seemed to be trying to relieve some of the anxiety of the moment—trying to be serious and funny at the same time, but it wasn't working as well as it had on previous occasions. He sensed this, and I decided to break through the tension on my own.

"The Ark was meant to hold the tablets Moses brought down from Mount Sinai," I responded. "It's also said to have held Aaron's staff, as well as manna, the food God sent to the Israelites when they were lost in the desert. God communicated with Moses from between the two cherubim, the angels you see there at the top. There were, in fact, two different arks: the temporary one made by

Moses and a later more ornate version made by Bezalel. Wherever it went, it produced miracles, eventually becoming one of the most mysterious and sought after objects in history."

"Very good. Although there's a lot more to the Ark than meets the eye. It held far more than what we've been taught."

"Isn't it unusual to find a replica of the Ark in a Catholic church? Maybe something is hidden inside."

"Well, unless we develop x-ray vision or pry the lid off, we're not about to find out."

"I have the feeling that whatever is being held here isn't physical, but something different," I added, groping for a plausible answer.

"What makes you think that?"

"It's just a feeling I have, to be honest. I'm learning to trust that more as we move from place to place. I have the feeling that there are formulas or even codes here that, as you say, have energetically imprisoned a force of energy we don't necessarily want to deal with. That's the feeling I'm getting."

"Look straight up," Phil said, pointing to the ceiling.

I did as he asked and saw what he was pointing at: a single Templar cross was painted on the ceiling directly above the Ark. Lightning bolts surrounded the cross, giving it a strange, almost occult power.

"What do you think it means?" I asked.

"I'm not entirely sure, although I have my suspicions. There's something happening here that I don't fully understand. I've never felt anything like it before, although it's reminding me of something. It's a feeling I just can't shake."

That sounded familiar to me. "I'm experiencing the same thing. I keep feeling confusion . . . and pain. I'm also noticing something that I can't quite identify."

"Betrayal, maybe?"

"Yes, betrayal! I'm feeling betrayed. How did you know? Do you think it has something to do with the Ark?"

"Oh, I'm sure it's centered right here, in and around the Ark. It didn't start until we began chanting the name, so maybe whatever it is that we're feeling, we definitely had a hand in teasing it out. I suggest that we chant the name *El* 12 times, adding some special words each time—that is, if I can remember them all."

"I have to tell you the truth. This is making me a little nervous," I confessed. "I just hope it doesn't get worse."

"I think I have a handle on what it is we're dealing with here. What will happen is anybody's guess, but that's why we're here."

"Somehow that doesn't fill me with much confidence," I added in a low voice.

We stood in front of the Ark and closed our eyes. Phil continued, "I'm getting that we should continue chanting—not just the one name I chose for this church, but many. There's a power in this spot that cannot be released without harnessing more energy and strength than before. I'm going to chant many names, and you can simply respond after me. Understand?"

"Yes, I do."

"Okay, Jimmy. Repeat after me: *El Echad,* The One God."

"*El Echad,* The One God."

"*El Emet,* The God of Truth."

"*El Emet,* The God of Truth."

Phil continued chanting as I carefully recited the words back to him: "*El Shaddai,* All Sufficient God; *El Elyon,* Most High God; *El Gibbor,* Mighty God; *El Hashamayin,* The God of Heaven; *El Malei Rachamin,* All Merciful God; *El Rachum,* God of Compassion; *El Olam,* The Everlasting God; *El Channun,* The Gracious God; *El Yeshuatenu,* The God of Our Salvation; *El Tsaddik,* Righteous God; *Immanuel,* God Is in Us."

By the time we finished chanting the various names, I began feeling a familiar sensation. A strong sense of devotion—the same thing I felt when we were in the Church of the Assumption—began to wash over me. It was very much welcomed, given the confusion I was experiencing before. Then, almost as if I were dreaming, I saw her: the beautiful nun. I wasn't sure if I was actually seeing her with my eyes or somewhere deep within my own heart. She was radiant and dressed in a dazzling white garment, not the worn black habit she wore before. It was as if she had gone to Heaven and come back, and I wondered why she was there. She smiled at me and motioned for me to follow her. At first I didn't know what I should do. Phil's eyes were still closed, and I decided to step away from the Ark to see where she would lead me. It felt more like I was following a feeling than an apparition, but it felt completely real, as if she were really there walking directly in front of me.

We walked around the corner in the direction of the main altar. I wasn't sure where we were heading, but it seemed like she was floating a few inches off the ground instead of walking. She suddenly stopped and turned to face the altar. I came as close to her as I felt comfortable and then also turned to see what she was looking at. I couldn't believe that I hadn't noticed it before. At the rear of the altar, surrounded by enormous golden rays of light and ominous clouds, was the Tetragrammaton—YHWH. It was enclosed in a beautiful golden triangle and radiated its energy throughout the expansive church. She gazed at the name, then back at me. I realized that it was just on the other side of the wall from the Ark, under the Templar cross. I knew that Phil was still there, and I wondered how I was supposed to interpret this experience. Then the nun began floating back in the direction of the Ark, so I followed her once again.

When we arrived, Phil was still standing where I'd left him, but his eyes were now open. He didn't seem to see what I was seeing (or feeling), as if the nun was only visible to my eyes. He seemed lost in his own thoughts. Perhaps like me, he was having an experience that only he was privy to. It seemed that he was intently studying the Ark, and as I walked up to him, the nun stopped and turned to face it as well. Although I wasn't exactly sure what she was trying to communicate, I knew that it had something to do with the Tetragrammaton . . . and the Ark.

Was there some connection between the two? The Ark once held the Ten Commandments, Yahweh's covenant with Moses and the Israelites. But was there more? We had already chanted the name *Shaddai el Chai* as well as the additional ones. Perhaps adding Yahweh would push things over the edge. My only worry was that it might push *us* over the edge as well. The only thing that made me feel optimistic was the presence of the nun, and her radiance felt like the best defense from whatever might be inside.

"There's something I didn't see at the altar at first," I told Phil. "A Tetragrammaton is there, and I think we're supposed to use it to release whatever is inside the Ark."

"Yes, I knew it was there. But what makes you think—"

"The nun from the last church is here with us," I whispered. "She was dressed in black there, and now she's in white. I think I know why she's here."

We were all facing the Ark now: Phil, the nun, and me. At first, nothing seemed to be happening, but then it started. I began to feel waves of heat emanating from the Ark. The whole section of the church we were in seemed to be getting warmer. I also started to feel a slight vibration—like a train that was passing on a nearby track—and it remained at a steady pace. I looked over at Phil to see if he felt it, too, but he was standing there motionless with his eyes closed. I looked back at the Ark and saw a black haze forming over the cover, between the outstretched wings of the cherubim at the top of it. It startled me at first and I wanted to pull away, but something inside told me not to move.

The haze over the Ark increased. Within seconds, it had lifted away from the lid and was now hovering directly in front of us. It looked more silvery platinum in hue with what resembled rainbow-colored lights flashing through it. I felt a sudden rush of emotions, and I wanted to prod Phil out of his reverie or whatever it was he was experiencing, but something told me not to disturb him. I did, however, notice that he seemed to be humming softly, his lips barely moving.

I tried to make out what he was saying and finally realized that it was the Tetragrammaton. He was repeating the four letters over and over again, just under his breath. I decided to join him. A chorus of *"Yud Heh Vav Heh, Yud Heh Vav Heh"* rippled in waves toward the Ark, the vibration beginning to increase until it felt like the whole church was beginning to shake. I knew the sensation really wasn't happening except perhaps in my mind. But when I looked over at Phil, I noticed that his hands, which were gripping the railing, were moving almost imperceptibly, as though in response to some force or vibration. The haze began to lift higher over the Ark, and I immediately knew where it was heading—the golden Tetragrammaton. Just before the cloud disappeared into what seemed like a vortex spinning in the Tetragrammaton, all the emotions I was feeling seemed to blend into one distinct, unmistakable feeling: gratitude.

I looked over at where the nun had been and was almost unsurprised to see that she was no longer there. "Whatever it was, it's gone now," I said to Phil, whose gaze was still fixed on the radiant triangle with its golden rays. I noticed that his eyes were welling up with tears and realized that mine were as well.

"Anything from your nun?" he asked softly.

"No. She disappeared before the portal closed."

"Then I suggest we leave, too. Our work here is done."

We took a step back and turned away from the Ark. The air of the church was damp and cold, and I could think of nothing other than getting out of that place.

✧✧✧✧✧

CHAPTER 10

The Obelisk of Luxor

Adonai

I stopped on the steps of the church as we walked out the door. I needed to hold still, if only for a moment, as if it would somehow make me feel safer to be in a more familiar place, a world I could predict and understand. Whatever just happened, I didn't understand it, and it filled me with anxiety that I needed to shake before we moved on. Otherwise, I wasn't sure I'd be able to continue, and that was a possibility I didn't want to consider.

"Maybe we should talk about what happened," Phil finally said.

"Yes," I answered, taking a deep breath. "That's a great idea."

"Tell me your thoughts. What do you think that was all about?"

"I have no idea. I was hoping you'd tell me. Isn't that how this works . . . you orchestrate the adventure and then answer my questions when it's through? That's what I was hoping for, anyway."

"I'm not sure you'll like my answer—in fact, I'm not even sure I like it." There was a look on his face that frightened me, even more than the experience itself. It made me want to run back inside and reverse the direction of the last half hour, making it seem like it never happened at all.

I sat down on the wet steps. "That makes me feel even more uneasy."

"That's because it flies in the face of everything we've been taught. There are truths about the past we're going to need to confront sooner or later if we want to make sense of our lives and potential futures. I wish I had something more concrete for you right now, but I don't."

"So you're telling me that you don't know what it was that came out of the Ark? You're right—I don't like it."

"I'm not saying that, Jimmy. The truth is that I do have an idea of what happened back there and, more than that, *why* it happened. I just don't think that now is the time to go into it. I'd rather wait and see how things develop so I can be sure. I know that's difficult to hear, but I need you to trust me, trust yourself, and trust that all will be revealed at the proper time and place. There are some things that must remain mysteries to us, and I think this is one of them, for the time being at least . . . that is, until we reach a place of peace."

"What do you mean by a 'place of peace'?"

"All in good time. I do believe we're accomplishing what we've set out to do."

"Remind me what that was," I retorted, sounding more harsh than I'd intended.

"We are transforming ourselves through the Divine Names and, through us, everything we touch."

"It definitely did that."

"And we may need to leave it there. I suggest we continue on and move to our next location, which is just up the road."

"I'm not sure I'm okay with being in the dark like this," I added, as we started to walk again. "That was one of the most intense— and scary—experiences of my life. There has to be more you can tell me, something that will help me feel at ease."

Phil didn't say anything for several seconds, but it was long enough to increase the tension. "Like I said, when the time is right—all I'll say for now is that the places we've been to and the experiences we've shared seem to be leading toward something, some kind of—"

"Final encounter?"

"Well, I wouldn't use those words, but you're on the right track. *Confrontation* might be a little more accurate. Even so, there's no reason to make this any more menacing than it needs to be. I promise you that there's a method to this seeming madness . . . that it's part of a much larger plan."

I thought I saw a flash of uncertainty on Phil's face, as if he was trying to convince himself as much as me. It was time to move on, though, and I knew it. I'd have to be patient and wait for more information. We turned right when we came to the street and began walking down the Rue de Rivoli, one of the most famous thoroughfares in Paris, if not the world. "So, where are we going now?"

"We're going to one of the most storied locations in France," Phil replied. "It's a place where ancient mysteries and bloody histories collide, and that makes it a perfect candidate for the work we came here to do."

"I'm sure this city is full of places that match that description."

"Yes, but not like this one. To tell you the truth, I'm not exactly sure what to expect. I do know that where we're heading is an important link in the chain of events we're helping to create."

We turned off the Rue de Rivoli onto a lovely path framed by overhanging trees. We were walking along the edge of the Tuileries Gardens, which borders the Seine River, toward the Avenue des Champs-Élysées and the Arc de Triomphe. In the distance, I saw a large square with traffic running around a central point, and at the very center, I could see what looked like a needle rising into the sky. Phil seemed focused on the spot, walking with distinct purpose. "What's that place ahead of us?" I asked him.

"That's where we're headed. It's the largest and most famous public square in Paris—the Place de la Concorde. Situated along the Seine, it separates the Tuileries Gardens from the beginning of the Champs-Élysées. When it was built in the mid-1700s, it was called Place Louis XV and had a huge statue of the king riding a great stallion. From the square, you can turn around and see many of the most important and well-known places in the city, including the Eiffel Tower. And at the very center sits a potent pinnacle of power and ancient magic."

"That's the point I see in the middle of the square?"

"Yes, the Obélisque de Luxor at the Place de la Concorde—a pink granite monolith that was given to the French in 1829 by the viceroy of Egypt, Mehemet Ali. The obelisk, which once marked the entrance to the Temple of Amun-Mut-Khonsu at Luxor, is more than 3,300 years old and is decorated with hieroglyphics documenting the reigns of Ramses II and Ramses III."

"Ramses II was the Pharaoh whom Moses confronted," I added, finally grasping the connection.

"Let's just say that's what most people believe. Regardless, I'm getting a little ahead of myself. To more fully understand the significance of this amazing structure, you need to know what happened on the spot where it now stands. It served as a focal point for the bloodiest political upheaval in France's history—the French Revolution. When the revolutionaries seized power, they renamed the square Place de la Révolution and replaced the statue of Louis with a guillotine. Louis XVI and Marie Antoinette were executed there, among other notables. And in the summer of 1794 during the Reign of Terror, more than 1,300 people were beheaded there in public executions. People used to say that the stench of blood was so strong on the spot that cattle refused to cross the grounds. When it was known as the Place de Grève, convicted criminals were torn and dismembered alive for the entertainment of the reigning nobility and bourgeoisie of the time.

"Then came the Obelisk of Luxor and everything changed. It arrived during the winter solstice of 1833. Gilded images on the pedestal portray the monumental task of transporting the monolith to Paris and erecting it at the square. Rising to a height of 23 meters, it weighs over 230 tons, so you can imagine what it took, especially then."

"Makes one think about the building of the pyramids," I said. "They weren't afraid of grand projects."

"No, they certainly weren't. They were going to bring another obelisk but figured it was just too much work. This one stood for more than 33 centuries at the Temple of Luxor. Its capstone was believed to have been stolen in the 6th century. I'm hoping that a special way of looking at the hieroglyphics on the obelisk will help guide us on our journey."

"And that's why we're going there?" I inquired, almost with a sigh.

"That's why we're going there."

As we arrived at the square, I experienced the same feeling as when we approached Phil's other chosen 'power points'— fascination bordering on terror. Hundreds of people filled the area taking photographs in front of the obelisk or sitting on the steps enjoying a rare few moments of sunlight. I was still 30 or so meters away from the monolith when the hieroglyphics seemed to explode off the surface and penetrate my third eye. I stopped in my tracks and for several seconds felt as if I were paralyzed.

Phil quickly walked over to me. "Tell me what's happening."

"I don't know," I finally answered. "I can feel all this energy, but I'm not sure why."

"The other places we've visited seem to have opened you to the point that you respond almost immediately to their energy. I think you're starting to feel the hidden codes in the hieroglyphics—not intellectually, but energetically. I can feel it, too."

"Yes, but what does it mean?"

"That's what we're here to find out."

We walked toward the mysterious artifact, and as we did, the energy I felt softened. I started wondering if the day's excitement was beginning to get to me since I was now sensing ghosts and spirits lurking around every corner. I've always considered myself to be very discerning when it came to these things, but Phil's sense of drama was like a powerful tractor beam that pulled my awareness into his strange world of spirits, codes, and ancient magic.

The other possibility, however, was more likely to be true, and I knew it. As much as I wanted, perhaps even needed, Phil to be crazy, I knew his intuition was usually on target. In addition, what I felt and saw at the four churches we visited was real, and there was no way to argue it. I tried hard to convince myself otherwise, but the evidence was stacking up fast in favor of the impossible. I stepped toward the obelisk, and my knees weakened. After our experience with the Ark at Saint-Roch, I wasn't taking any unnecessary chances.

"What do you suggest we do here?" I asked tentatively.

"We'll do the same thing we've been doing at the other locations." Phil sensed my nervousness. "Don't worry about things going in the direction of Saint-Roch. As I've said, we're here primarily for the continuing education of our souls. Please don't forget that. We're going to call upon another of the Sacred Names of God, but not for any purpose other than to transform our own consciousness. In doing so, we'll have an effect on everything around us . . . every person and every situation because that's how grace works. It's the Moses Code in action again. As we free ourselves, the promise of liberation is extended to all of creation. This is the only thing we're here to do. I can't overemphasize how important this is to remember."

"I remember."

"I suggest we have a seat on the ledge." Phil pointed toward the enormous spear. "It may be the only time we feel sunlight today."

We walked toward the obelisk and sat down on the wet granite. A young French couple was kissing only a few feet away from us, and a Japanese family was busy taking pictures of each other on the other side. I tried to focus on the cars that spun around the square, the incredible buildings that lined the boulevard, anything other than the fear I felt. Phil must have noticed this and nudged me with his arm. "Did you hear what I just said?" he asked.

"No, I spaced out for a minute."

"The next name we're going to call on is one of the most powerful, and that's why I wanted to use it here. The name is *Adonai,* meaning 'Lord.' Along with *Elohim,* it's used in place of the Tetragrammaton. As we've discussed, it's common practice to substitute terms of reverence rather than uttering the unspeakable Holy Name."

"Didn't we already use this in place of the Tetragrammaton when we were at Sacré-Coeur?"

"It's important to remember that the names we're using, in one fashion, simply represent Divine Natures or attributes. They relate to aspects of ourselves, to our own Divinely inspired natures that we bring to light when we repeat them. And yes, we did use it at Sacré-Coeur, but now we'll use it on its own . . . not in substitution for anything else."

I tried to listen intently as Phil was speaking, but there seemed to be something drawing my attention to the obelisk.

"A common variation of this name as it applies to the Kabbalistic Tree of Life is *Adonai Melekh ha Aretz,* meaning 'Lord-King of the Earth.'" Phil continued, "Actually, let's use that. If my suspicions are correct, this is the best choice."

"What suspicions?" I asked, with more than a hint of curiosity.

"It's hard to say what form of consciousness we're going to encounter here. The energy of this place is unlike anywhere we've been. Remember, this obelisk used to stand at the Temple of Luxor, situated along the Nile in Egypt. The true name is the Temple of Amun-Mut-Knonsu, representing the 'temple of man.' It's literally an alchemical text in stone, encoding a vast and sophisticated knowledge of sacred spiritual science and power lost to most of us in the mists of antiquity. We've got to be ready with both barrels loaded."

"I just hope that doesn't end up being an accurate analogy."

"Just remember what I keep telling you: we're not here to use the names to release anything other than the chains around our own souls. To do anything else would be truly blasphemous. It would be tantamount to using the Holy Names of God in vain, so to speak. We want to stay clear, focused, and in the highest integrity—agreed?"

"Agreed."

We closed our eyes and took several deep breaths, using them to drown out the noise and traffic. Phil said something about Dorothy's silver slippers (I don't remember exactly what it was) and did a somewhat longer than usual protection ritual. Then, using our finger-counting system, we began chanting the name: *"Adonai Melekh ha Aretz, En Sof; Adonai Melekh ha Aretz, En Sof; Adonai Melekh ha Aretz, En Sof . . ."*

Just as we had done four times previously, we chanted the name 12 times and let it sink deep into our consciousness. When we were finished, Phil looked over at me. "There are two things I need to say to you: I don't want you to get too far away from me this time. I'm not trying to scare you, but, like I said before, there's very ancient magic at work here, possibly a form we haven't yet encountered. It may surprise us."

"I haven't stopped being surprised since we began. What's the second thing?"

"I have a suggestion about how to focus on the obelisk's hieroglyphics. It's an ancient way of looking at encoded material and letting your soul unlock the mysteries, instead of your mind. I don't know if it will work here, but it's worth trying. It's called *stereogrammatic vision.* Remember the Magic Eye books that were popular in the 90s? The principle is similar. The books featured autostereograms, which allowed people to see three-dimensional images on two-dimensional surfaces. In other words, one could see hidden patterns within the images. The process is somewhat related to what's called *stereoscopic vision.* You let your eyes go out of focus, allowing them to cross slightly. The builders of ancient temples were well aware of this process, I assure you. Use this special technique for looking at the hieroglyphics, and we'll see what happens."

"And what should I do if I see something?" I asked.

"Come and get me. I'll do the same and find you if I see something. Just stay close."

We walked in different directions until we stood on opposite sides of the obelisk. At first I didn't know what to do but stood gazing at the intricate designs, hoping something would jump out at me. It didn't. I tried to blend in with all the other tourists around me, not wanting to seem too strange. I decided to look at the obelisk using the process Phil showed me. I started to feel silly, until I looked over to the other side of the monument and saw Phil squinting and tilting his head back and forth. A young woman giggled as she walked past him. It actually took the pressure off of me for a moment, so I focused on the writing once again and began looking at the hieroglyphics as Phil had suggested.

"Let me see something here that makes sense," I uttered beneath my breath, hoping the symbols and Egyptian letters would suddenly spring to life and realign themselves in English. The illusion of movement could easily be created by crossing my eyes too far, but the physical discomfort this caused seemed to cancel out any potential benefits. I stood in front of each side of the obelisk hoping for something to happen, and it wasn't until I tested the fourth side that something seemed to stir inside me. At first it felt like a flutter in my stomach, but then the feeling increased until it was in my throat. I stood rooted in place holding my gaze, waiting for something more. A minute passed and the sensation I felt seemed to grow stronger, but still no message.

Finally, I let my gaze release its grip on the tower, and I looked down at my feet. I noticed I was standing directly on something carved into the sidewalk. I took a step back and realized that a Templar cross had been etched into the cement when it was originally laid, and the uncomfortable feeling in my body seemed to dissipate when I wasn't standing directly on top of the symbol. I stepped back again and the feeling returned. I looked over at Phil until he caught my eye, and I waved for him to come over.

"What's happening?"

"I think I discovered something. Someone carved a Templar cross into the cement, and when I stand on it, I feel the strangest sensations."

"Let me try." Phil stood on the cross and closed his eyes. "Wow, I can feel it, too. It's like currents of energy running through my feet and up my legs into my solar plexus."

"I felt something similar. What do you think it means?"

"Give me a moment. . . ." Phil began squinting and crossing his eyes as he looked up toward the obelisk. He stood on the cross staring at the obelisk for at least a minute, then closed his eyes and looked at me. "I was chanting the name as I looked and something seemed to happen. Here, you try it, and tell me what you see."

Phil stepped to the side of the symbol, and I replaced him. I took a deep breath and then began to chant *"Adonai Melekh ha Aretz, En Sof"* in a soft voice. At first nothing seemed to change on the obelisk, and I wondered if it was another dead end. Then I noticed something shift in the corner of my eye, almost as if the Egyptian letters were rearranging themselves. For a second, I lost my focus and when I looked back at the monument, I realized that nothing had changed at all. But when I let my focus fade again, the sensation returned.

The symbols seemed to morph, and I knew they were trying to communicate something to me—not with words as much as through my unconscious mind. I recalled the movie *A Beautiful Mind* and how John Nash used to see letters come right off the pages of newspapers. I wondered if the same process was at work here. The possibility of translating what I saw into normal words seemed impossible in that moment, and yet I understood on a deeper level that a conversation was taking place deep within me. Even in the midst of the experience, I questioned whether it was real or in my imagination, although the feeling that I was actually communicating with something that was attached to the obelisk—a spirit or some kind of ancient entity—suddenly felt more than plausible.

"You feel thy presence?" it seemed to ask.

"I'm not really sure," I responded in my own mind, sure that whatever was speaking through me would understand. *"I'm taking all this as it comes."*

"Who art thou, and why do thou disturb me?"

"Who are you and why are you here?" I asked.

"Thou canst fathom not who I am, but why I am here thou art beginning to understand, though thou grasp is that of a primitive mind."

I didn't know whether or not to feel insulted. Then again, I was the one talking to an obelisk.

"I have been here longer than thou canst imagine, and my power,

though faded with time, is still great. I can create or destroy. What wouldst thou have me do?"

I lost my focus for a moment, wondering again if it was all in my mind. I looked over at Phil. "What's happening?" he asked.

"I'm not really sure. It's like I'm talking to someone, or something, imprisoned in the obelisk, but I'm not sure what it is or even if it's actually happening."

"Just stay with it and trust your intuition. I have the feeling you're on to something."

I closed my eyes for a few seconds and then let my gaze return to the obelisk. At the top was a cap made of gold leaf, which only added to its allure. The voice returned almost immediately: *"What wouldst thou have of me?"*

"Nothing. We are here to help. We are here to chant the name of God."

"'The name of God,' sayest you. And which God wouldst thou be calling?"

"We're calling upon the One God who is known by many names."

A high-pitched laugh began reverberating in my head. *"Who is the one thou wouldst call?"*

In a barely audible voice, I said: "We call upon Adonai, the Lord of the Universe. We have been called to stand in this spot and speak to you. The Lord wants you to know that you do not need to stay here. You have been bound to this structure for thousands of years; you have been taken to this foreign land, and you have become confused. But you do not need to stay. Through the power of the Sacred Name Adonai, I call upon you to be released from this bondage, all this magic, and return to your Source."

I felt a wave of searing heat hit my face that nearly knocked me backward. Then I heard Phil speaking with urgency. "Stop, Jimmy!" he exclaimed. "This is all wrong."

The voice resumed in my head: *"Who is he?"*

"He is my friend, a friend who understands this better than I do," I offered, not sure whether bringing Phil in at that particular moment was a good idea. Phil was looking at me with a mixed look of utter disbelief and compassion.

"Jimmy, please stop," he repeated, in a low voice very close to my ear. "Please don't use the names like that. How do you know it doesn't belong here?"

I willed myself to turn away from the tower. "Belong here? What do you mean?"

"It may belong here. How are we to know? Just because whatever it is *is* here, it doesn't mean that it doesn't belong—that it isn't part of the plan."

Just then I remembered what Phil had told me earlier: that Paris means at the 'feet of Isis.' At that moment, I felt a wave of relief wash over me and also something else . . . understanding. I felt a voice inside my head say *thank you,* and I nearly collapsed on the spot as blood rushed into my brain.

Suddenly, just as it all started, it was over. I listened and heard no voice. I searched my feelings and felt nothing, except perhaps relief. The symbols and letters seemed to settle again inside the stone giant. I turned to Phil, and he was smiling at me.

"Did you feel any of that?" I asked, regaining my balance.

"Any of what? I'm not sure what happened. I felt you going deep, but I couldn't follow. When I heard you make that command in the name of *Adonai,* I tried to stop you."

Phil listened intently as I told him about the conversation as well as the energy I felt. "Do you think it's even possible?" I asked. "It's more likely that I'm making things up in my head because of everything that has already gone down." I blurted this out to convince myself as much as Phil.

"I have no way of telling you if you made it up. Of course, it's possible—anything's possible—but it's also possible that what took place has a basis in reality . . . although not this reality."

We sat down on one of the embankments lining the square. "Think about it," he said. "Whatever it is, we have no idea how long it's been here or where it's from. Maybe it's been here all along. Lord knows the magic it has witnessed, possibly at its own command. And then there's the plaza, a powerful vortex of its own. Think about all the terrible *and* wonderful things that have happened right here where we sit. Think about the guillotine and the couple kissing. As I said before, anything is possible."

"But there doesn't seem to be any kind of conclusion. I thought we were here to release entities and send them into the light."

"No, Jimmy. We're here to release ourselves into the light. Anything that wants to come along for the ride is more than welcome."

"Do you think it's still here?"

"I honestly don't know. And I really don't think that's the point anymore. Do you?" Phil closed his eyes and raised his hands as if to feel something that his normal senses might otherwise miss. He stood that way for at least a minute and then turned to me. "We should go."

"Go? Why? What just happened?"

Phil took me by the arm, and we started walking away from the square. "Sometimes things are better left undisturbed," he replied, picking up the pace. "All I know is that regardless of whatever it was you felt, it either doesn't want or need to leave—or is unable to leave—and it's beyond our expertise to know one way or the other."

"I'm getting the impression that you're afraid." The thought alone made me even more scared.

"I'm not really afraid. I've just been around long enough to know when it's time to throw in the towel."

"You mean give up?"

"No, Jimmy, I mean surrender."

I turned to look at the obelisk. At that moment, the sun disappeared behind a cloud, making it look dark and foreboding. The light drizzle returned, and a shadowy energy filled the entire square, yet I felt very much at peace.

"This is the Place de la Concorde, the Place of Peace, after all. Let's move on to the next location." Phil smiled as he spoke. We gazed at the towering monument one last time and started walking toward the Eiffel Tower.

"Yes, let's. I couldn't agree more."

CHAPTER 11

The Final Grand Master

Elohim Gibor

"**I** don't know whether to doubt all the things that are happening or to believe them."

We were a block away from the Obelisk of Luxor, walking back along the Rue de Rivoli, and I wasn't sure I wanted to continue. After five paranormal adventures, I was almost convinced that my imagination had finally gotten the best of me. There was very little I could point to that didn't seem to end with one definite conclusion: I'd made it all up in my head. In a way it made me feel better, as if I were off the hook and wouldn't need to continue exorcising the demons and spirits of Paris. The fact was that I felt overwhelmingly relieved.

"Only you know if you've imagined everything," Phil remarked. "Even if I told you that what you've been experiencing was real and that you've played a very important role at each stop on this little journey of ours, you would still need to decide for yourself what was and wasn't real."

"Is that what you're telling me?"

"I'm telling you that the power in each of the Sacred Names is very real, and when you open to their power, they have the potential to transform you on the deepest levels imaginable. What happens after that is the mystery. I've never claimed we were using them to do anything other than—"

"'To open the seals within our own hearts and souls to let grace flow into and through us.' Yes, I remember. But you can't blame me for freaking out a bit. This is pretty far outside my normal box."

"It's outside my box, too," Phil said as we turned a corner onto Pont Neuf. He explained that the bridge we were now on was the oldest standing bridge that spanned the Seine in all of Paris. "I told you I've never done anything quite like this before. There's a part of me that's amazed at what's happening—same as you. But I know it isn't in my imagination. I'm convinced that it has all been very real."

We stopped at a statue of Henry IV mounted on a horse. Then Phil led me down a winding stone staircase that opened up into a public park called the Parc Vert Gallant. The grassy area was long and narrow, flanked with well-manicured shrubs and benches that ran the entire distance of the park. We continued down the stairs until we reached the bottom, and Phil motioned for me to stop.

"Welcome to the Île de la Cité. This island is the geographic center of all of Paris—and its heart in medieval times." Phil pointed toward three stone pillars behind me, between which were twin stairwells. Near the top of the central pillar a few feet above our heads, an iron plaque was bolted to the wall that read:

A CET ENDROIT
JACQUES DE MOLAY
DERNIER GRAND MAÎTRE
DE L'ORDRE DU TEMPLE
A ÉTÉ BRÛLÉ LE 18 MARS 1314

"At this location, Jacques de Molay, last Grand Master of the Knights Templar, was burned on March 18, 1314," Phil read. "Île de la Cité is only one of two natural islands in the Seine within the city of Paris. It used to be called Île des Javiaux or Île aux Juifs and was home to the original inhabitants of Paris, the Parisii. And it was here at this location that Jacques de Molay, 23rd and last Grand Master of the Knights Templar, along with Geoffroy de Charney, was burned at the stake in the shadow of the Convent of St. Augustine. Just like it says on the plaque, more or less."

I looked at the plaque and then back at Phil. "Jacques de Molay," I repeated. "I knew the name sounded familiar."

"Anyone who hasn't been living in a cave for the past several years has heard the name Jacques de Molay. Most people nowadays are somewhat familiar with the story of the Knights Templar, especially since the publication of *The Da Vinci Code.*"

Phil was right. The popularity of Dan Brown's magnum opus reignited worldwide interest in the exploits of the controversial Templars, as well as giving millions of people their first glance at this mysterious order of monastic warrior-knights. The book *Holy Blood, Holy Grail* had done the same back in the early '80s.

"Why was de Molay brought here to be burned?"

"King Philip IV of France, also known as Philippe le Bel, along with Pope Clement V, orchestrated the Templars' downfall. At that time, if you'll recall, the Louvre served as the Palace Complex. Having it done here provided Philip with an excellent view from his palace window. You see, Philip himself tried to gain admission to the Order. He thought that in time he could possibly become a Grand Master and control or subvert it from the inside. When he was denied admission, he began in earnest to plot its demise. He even named de Molay as godfather to his son in order to gain favor with the Order. This is not very well known. You see, Philip had borrowed a ton of money from the Templars to finance his war on England. De Molay was also one of the pallbearers at the funeral of Philip's sister-in-law. This was on October 12, 1307. The very next day, Friday the 13th, just about every Templar in France, including de Molay, was under arrest."

"This is really fascinating."

"On November 22, 1307, Pope Clement issued his papal bull *Pastoralis Praeeminentiae,* directing all Christian monarchs throughout Europe to arrest all members of the Order and impound their assets, which were considerable. This, in effect, was the death knell for the Templars. The nail in the coffin was, of course, the papal bull *Vox in Excelso* of April 3, 1312, which declared the Templars suppressed, officially dissolving the Order."

"I'm guessing that canceled King Philip's debt to the Templars," I added.

"That's right. And de Molay, along with Geoffroy de Charney, received the harshest punishment the king could unleash, and this was after years of horrendously brutal torture and duress, in which they and countless other Templars confessed to all manner of blasphemous acts. By the way, when you're being burned at the stake, you hope they build a very large fire. That way the carbon monoxide in the smoke kills you before the flames ever touch your skin. If they build a small fire, like they did here, you literally roast over a long period of time. You might say that de Molay and de Charney died as martyrs, even though they didn't die in battle, which to the Templars was a great honor and guaranteed them a place in Heaven."

"Weren't documents found that exonerated the Templars?"

"Yes—in 2001 or 2002, I believe. Dr. Barbara Frale, a medievalist at the Secret Vatican Archives, discovered what's known as the 'Chinon Parchment.' It was found due to a filing error—isn't that amazing? It proved that Pope Clement secretly pardoned the Order in 1314."

"How do you know all this?"

"Let's just say that my application to view the Secret Archives has been tied up in a lot of red tape for some time . . . I'm not holding my breath."

"I can't even imagine you loose in the Vatican Archives," I quipped. "So the Templars weren't the heretics they were made out to be?"

"To be perfectly honest, there's no simple answer to that question. According to church dogma, their beliefs would certainly be regarded as heretical. As far as their practices, well, that's a horse of yet another color. Spitting on the cross, denying the crucifixion, and other 'acts of abomination' they were accused of are still the subject of hot debate in various circles. So many of the mysteries of the Templars are tied up in intrigue and the pursuit of vested interests. Many will remain mysteries. The truth can seem like heresy to the one who is afraid of the truth, if you know what I mean."

"That's an unbelievable story, but I'm wondering why you felt this would be an appropriate place for us to work with the Divine Names."

"I chose this location for two reasons," Phil contended. "First, because this island is the center of Paris—a very powerful vortex and the home of the Parisii. That's enough in and of itself."

"What's the other reason?"

"The second reason is that the Sacred Name I want to use here is especially appropriate for this spot. It's *Elohim Gibor,* meaning 'Heavenly Warrior' or 'God of Battles.'"

"We usually don't want to think of God as a warrior, or leading heavenly armies into battle, but I believe it's important," I interjected. "When we speak of God, we're not talking about a person or an entity that has some qualities but not others. We're talking about the complete summation of everything that exists, which includes many of the parts of ourselves we would rather deny. God is lover and warrior in one, as well as every other aspect."

"Yes, you could say that *Elohim Gibor* represents the warrior aspect of God. The name corresponds to Geburah on the Kabbalistic Tree of Life: to severity, judgment, justice, harsh action, and—are you ready for this one—defending innocence." Phil smiled broadly, knowing he'd just scored a direct hit. "De Molay recanted his forced confession at the burning, restated his innocence, and asked that his hands could be freed so that he could pray to the Virgin Mary. He had asked to be tied facing the Cathedral of Notre-Dame, which stands on the opposite end of the Île de la Cité. He prayed as the flames engulfed him, and his ashes were scattered on the Seine.

"By the way, I read where Geburah is also associated with fire in the respect of a ceremonial burning as form of purification. And if that wasn't enough, images that are commonly associated with the sphere of Geburah are the sword and the flame. Pretty appropriate, wouldn't you agree?"

"This seems very different from the other spots we've visited," I added. "I don't get the sense that de Molay is here. Do you?"

"I do feel there's something here for us and that the name will reveal it. In all the places we've visited so far, we've looked for certain signs or symbols that confirmed we were on the right track. So far we've been guided by Templar crosses and images of the Divine Feminine, as well as the Tetragrammaton."

"You said this place is an energetic vortex. Maybe we'll find something here, some energy signature that stops energy from flowing. That's what happens when a house or a place is haunted, right? Something locks the energy in place so that it can't move on. If that's happening here, we can use the name to heal the rift and release whatever is holding it in place."

"What makes you so sure that anything needs to be released?" Phil asked. "Why do you think the place is haunted?"

"Why else would we be here? I'm sure you didn't bring me here just to sightsee. What do you suggest we do?"

"As before, let's begin by chanting the name and then let Spirit move us wherever we need to be. If I'm right, then something will happen. It may be subtle or obvious, but it will be there nonetheless."

We looked over to one side of the park and spotted several benches against the water. We walked over and sat down. I took hold of my left hand and felt for the first knuckle. With my fingers in place, we began our chant.

"Let's hope that our prayers pass through the Gate of Tears," Phil remarked.

"The Gate of Tears?"

"Let's just say I believe that someone is always listening. Let's begin."

He hadn't answered my question, but I decided to let it pass for the moment: *"Elohim Gibor, En Sof; Elohim Gibor, En Sof; Elohim Gibor, En Sof . . ."*

When we finished, I expected to feel a change in the air, as if a sudden wind would rise or the Seine would send a thick wave crashing against the shore, spilling onto the grass and sidewalk.

Nothing happened. I looked over at Phil, but his eyes were still closed, and I wondered what I should do. I finally stood up and began walking slowly to the far side of the island, a small point with steel railings to keep visitors from wandering onto the rocks and into the water. I stood there for a moment watching a glass-covered boat pass by, filled with assorted tourists completely unaware of the tragedy that took place on this tiny stretch of land 700 years ago. Why would they care that two innocent men had been tortured in the most hideous manners imaginable and burned alive? The fact that I was standing on the spot where de Molay was killed made it feel very real, and I wanted to experience it for all it was worth.

I turned and walked back in the other direction, back where I saw Phil still sitting on the bench. As I walked, I looked around in the grass and flower beds, hoping to find a symbol or sign that would give us an additional reason for being there. If one had been placed on the island hundreds of years ago, it could be covered now, perhaps hidden beneath a shrub or somewhere else the eyes wouldn't instantly perceive it. I expected to find a Templar cross, perhaps one that was placed there to honor the martyred Templars. I looked for at least 15 minutes, but in the end there was nothing that drew my attention. I headed back over to Phil.

"There's nothing here," I said to him.

"What do you mean?"

"There are no signs or anything similar to the other places we've been to. I thought there would be, but there isn't."

"It's here. You just haven't been looking in the right place."

"What do you mean?"

Phil stood up and we walked back toward the stone pillars and the plaque dedicated to the last Grand Master of the Templars. "I want you to imagine de Molay. Think about what he might have looked like—a long white mantle worn over his armor and the one thing that would have stood out more than anything else. Can you guess what it is?"

I thought for a moment, jogging my memory to evoke images of Templar Knights I'd seen in books and films. Then it hit me. "The cross. You would see the red cross on the front of his tunic."

"Exactly! The *croix pattée*. The blood sacrifice of the lamb of God and the enduring mystery of Christ's blood. In *Dialogue with Trypho,* Saint Justin Martyr talks about the lamb, which the law prescribed to have roasted whole. You see, de Molay's cross is our cross. You've been looking for Templar symbolism in the grass, the flowers, the shrubbery . . . but it's all around us."

"You mean the spirit of de Molay himself."

"That's correct. His spirit is everywhere here, and that's why we came—to honor all genuine guardians of the Grail and all seekers of the truth, as well as those who died protecting and preserving the truth. We're all children of the Grail, Jimmy. The true Grail is inside each and every one of us. The quest for the Grail is the greatest of all spiritual endeavors: it's the quest for the eternal in ourselves and a deeper connection to the Source of all creation. We aren't here to release or exorcise anything at all. It's all about our return to innocence. It's about the confessions we've made under duress and how we are washed clean in the light of grace."

"Yes, I can feel it. I didn't recognize it in that way, but now that you say that . . . yes."

"And that's all that really matters. The Holy Names of God are simply to help us wake up to the holiness within. When that happens, then the dramas and the fictions we weave around our lives simply lose their significance. I'm certain that the gates of Heaven opened wide to receive de Molay that fateful day."

Phil began walking up the staircase back toward the street. I followed, but stopped momentarily to take a last look at the plaque; and for the first time since we began earlier that morning, I felt light and deeply satisfied.

✧✧✧✧✧

CHAPTER 12

Notre-Dame Cathedral

Elohim Tzabaoth

I'd visited the cathedral once before many years earlier, but the sight of it in the distance still aroused such energy and emotion in me. The stories of Victor Hugo, of the Hunchback and the French Revolution, immediately sprang into my mind. The two enormous bell towers filled me with an overwhelming desire to stop and absorb its transforming beauty. The square in front of the cathedral was filled with tourists and street performers from every corner of the globe, and the line of saints looking down upon them from just above the ancient doors seemed glad to have them. It's a sight like none other in Paris—or the world, for that matter—and for a moment, it made me forget why I was there, other than taking in the sheer majesty of the place.

"It's awe inspiring, isn't it?" Phil remarked.

"Amazing. It makes me wonder how anything sinister could be lurking here."

"There's nothing sinister about it," he answered. "There's nothing intrinsically sinister about any of these places, no matter how things may appear. Nothing is lying in wait for innocent souls to come passing by. On the other hand, we sometimes do invite these energies through our own choice *not* to acknowledge them. This can be conscious or unconscious. The way scenarios like this play out is more a matter of the latter, so to speak. Many of these energies are like lost orphans—not so different from the way a lot of us feel. They've been magnetized to a world not of their choosing . . . in many cases by misguided magical intent, often by agreement. They're not evil or bad; they just don't belong here.

"Please don't get me wrong. I'm not saying there aren't sinister energies out there. Regardless, the only thing we're required to do is love them and love ourselves enough to let them go, and sometimes that requires tough love. If we went in thinking we were entering a battle, then we would be inviting one. Trust me, these are not the kind of forces you want to do battle with, or otherwise mess with. It's a fight you'd be fated to lose. But if we enter with open hearts, a genuine desire to serve, and protected fields, then the reception we'll receive here, and in similar places, will be very different."

Considering the gargoyles that lined the roof of nearly the entire structure, these were interesting words. And yet I had to agree with him. After visiting six different locations and encountering a number of strange and bizarre energies, I realized that there was nothing demonic or evil about any of them. As Phil had said, they seemed trapped in a world they didn't know how to escape from, and we came with an answer, an answer to *their* prayers.

We seem to petition the angels for guidance and assistance in times of need, but I guess it may also work the other way. Maybe they need us just as much as we need them. After all, they're part of us just as we are of each other. More and more this mission, and my life, was beginning to make sense. The Holy Names we brought did seem to contain profound and particular energies with the power to transform. And as Phil kept repeating, the only person I had to really be concerned with was me. As I transformed, everything around me had the potential to transform. It's about individual choice.

"I think I want to know the name we'll be chanting before we go inside," I said to him. "I don't really know why. Maybe because there will be too many people once we're in there . . . I'm really not sure. We can still chant in the cathedral, but do you mind?"

"I was just thinking the same thing . . . good to know that our thoughts are on the same lines. There are an awful lot of people inside. It will be nice to get the discussion out of the way now, and then we can do the chant once we're in the cathedral."

Three steps lined the street moving away from the main doors of Notre-Dame, so we found a spot away from the largest groups and sat down. The rain fell like a gentle mist covering the people and everything around us like a baptism, and I felt the wetness from the cement as I found my place. It didn't feel strange at all that we were there, as if the multiplicity of the throng blended with the diverse emotions I was feeling within myself.

"Okay," Phil started as he opened his notebook. "The name we're going to use here is *Elohim Tzabaoth,* meaning 'God of Hosts' or 'God's Host of Armies.' It's related to the Hod on the Tree of Life, which is itself associated with *Din,* the Hebrew word for the Divine attribute of justice. This name also has associations with Archangel Michael, the *B'nai Elohim,* the 'Sons and Daughters of Light,' and the 'Givers of Pain and Delight,' but not in a *Star Trek* sense."

"You know, I'm pretty sure I've heard this name before, and I think it was in some magical context."

"It's not really magic at issue here," Phil replied, adjusting himself in his seat, more for dramatic effect than comfort. "In truth, we're all magicians at heart. Aleister Crowley was on the right track when he said that 'magick is the science and art of causing change to occur in conformity with will.' When you think about it, it's really one of the major themes of the Moses Code. I think the message, and the great power of using the Code, is just that—to effect change by the use of will, the right and proper use of will. Take the name 'I AM THAT, I AM.' The more precise definition is 'I will be what I will be,' or even more accurately, 'I am in the process of becoming what I will myself to be.' It's all about choice and the exercise of our wills."

"Yes, I see that," I said.

"I'm glad you do. Like I said before, the object of all spiritual practice, including magic, is to deepen one's relationship with the Source of All Things, to God. In true spiritual practice, you dedicate your life to understanding the true nature of the Divine, leading, of course, to the central mystery of yourself.

"According to most Kabbalists, we cannot yet understand the infinity of God. We can only fathom the unfathomable through his creations. As we come to know ourselves, we come to know more of God. We come to know God through our experience of God. Through the ages, systems of magic have been passed down to us, or maybe even brought up to us, allowing us to evoke very powerful spiritual energies . . . energies that can be used, or abused, according to the will of the magical operator. I'm sure you've heard of Enochian magic."

"Yeah, I have. Tell me more."

"Enochian magic is a system of summoning and commanding spiritual energies (mainly in the form we know as 'angelic energies') that was brought through most recently in the late 16th century. This system employs a language known as Enochian, the same language that was taught to the biblical patriarch Enoch by the same class of angels."

"What do you mean by a *class* of angels?"

"Fallen angels, to be precise, or so it is believed," Phil said with a half smile. "These angels are said to watch over humanity from the four Watchtowers of Creation. Enochian magic is designed to literally open the *locked gates* of these great Watchtowers, which are said to stand guard against the chaos that lies at the outer extremities of our Universe."

"Doesn't this have something to do with Dr. John Dee?" I asked. "I remember reading about this. He was a close confidant of Elizabeth I, and some actually suspect he had something to do with the storm that destroyed the Spanish Armada."

"That's right," Phil confirmed, almost surprised that I was aware of the connection.

"So, what was the purpose of these Enochian calls?"

"It's from these Watchtowers that these angels can be summoned into this world by means of the Enochian systems. There are many hierarchies and orders of spiritual intelligence in the Universe that can be made to do our bidding, although there's usually a price to be paid."

"You mean our souls?"

"Perhaps, if you believe your Bible stories. The important thing to remember is that it's not magic that's at fault here. It's not the fault of the system per se, but more a matter of how the system is used. It's all about consciousness and intent. I'm talking about misguided souls who, in a self-serving quest for power or control, let loose spiritual energies on this planet that were never meant to wander the earth freely. That's why many of these cathedrals were built—to attract and trap them until such time as they could be guided home. Lots of other energies get trapped in places like this as well. We'll talk more about them at our next stop. Much of the strife and pain that exist in the world today is on account of these energies being present."

I was feeling a little confused and needed some clarity. "I don't understand, Phil. This is something I've been meaning to ask you since we began. Now is as good a time as any. How is it that spiritual energies can be negative or evil?"

"Spirit is spirit, Jimmy," he replied, as if he were a high-school teacher. "Everything is composed of spirit, of particles, units of the consciousness of God. It's like someone calling themselves an 'energy healer,' as if there were something else we use to heal with. It's simply energy. It's the intention that gives it its direction. Crowley also said that every intentional act is an act of magic. It's all spirit, all consciousness, all God."

I thought about what Phil was saying, and I felt myself beginning to comprehend his words on deeper levels. I began to think about all of my experiences—all the lessons I'd been taught in my adventures and how they were beginning to make even more sense given the context of what we were doing. I thought about the world at large and why peace seems so elusive. Could it really be true that these energies contribute to the hatred and negativity manifesting in the world today?

At the same time, I remembered what *A Course in Miracles* says, that everything is either a call for love or an act of love. Phil must have sensed what I was thinking and feeling. He spoke more softly and in measured tones. "When we chant the names, we're opening ourselves up to grace flowing into and through us. This *field of grace* acts like a beacon of light, illuminating the portals so that these energies can find their way back from where they came. This is the time of prophesy, Jimmy. The dimensions are blending and the gates are opening like never before. It's a perfect opportunity to light the way home. Even the devotional systems of St. Francis of Assisi are thought to encode vast alchemical secrets. What do you think of that?"

"I find that hard to believe, but go on."

"Why do you find that so hard to believe? You don't think it's possible that St. Francis was privy to some of these codes and secrets, or that he might have been able to see past the veils through his devotional practices and meditations?"

"I really don't want to get too off track on a discussion about St. Francis. I'd really rather hear more about Enochian magic."

"Suit yourself," Phil replied, almost disappointed that I didn't want to spar with him. "Enochian is an extremely complex and sophisticated system of magic. There are many others that have a bearing on the work we're doing here. I could go down a list for you, but that would only bog you down with lots of information. I'll mention a few, though."

I wanted to hear more, but I was also conscious of the time. There was still a lot of work to do, and we needed to be getting inside.

Phil noticed my impatience. "We'll go inside in a minute. I just want to finish this thought. Here are some of the other forms of magic that are related: there is *The Lesser Key of Solomon, The Heptameron, The Necronomicon, The Sacred Magic of Abra-Melin the Mage,* and many others. And then there are the *grimoires,* magical workbooks that were written expressly for use by Catholic priests."

"Catholic priests?" I gasped, suddenly reengaged.

"Yes, but that's definitely something we'll need to put on the back burner for the time being. Time, as you said, is of the essence."

"Yes, but why did you feel the need to tell me all this? What's the greatest threat to us regarding these misplaced energies?"

"Well, the first thing that comes to mind is the electromagnetic balance of the planet," Phil answered. "Especially at this critical juncture . . . so much change is taking place, changes that are absolutely unprecedented in our recorded history. I'm talking about the shifts we're in the midst of, right here and now. I'll fill you in more later. We should probably be making our way inside."

"But what does the electromagnetic balance of the planet have to do with magical systems . . ." By the time I finished my question, Phil was up and walking. I caught up to him, and we joined the line that snaked its way to the primary entrance.

"What can you tell me about the history of Notre-Dame?" I asked as we moved slowly toward the door.

"Well, there's so much I'm not really sure where to begin. Most historians believe there were pagan churches and temples here on this island for hundreds, even thousands, of years before Christianity finally took hold. Then sometime around the 4th century, an enormous basilica with five naves was built to resemble the ancient basilicas of Rome. It was dedicated to Saint Stephen, and its western façade was located about 40 meters west of the current Notre-Dame.

"It remained there for hundreds of years until the 12th century, when, during the rule of Louis VII, a new cathedral much larger than St. Stephen's was built according to the Gothic style that was gaining popularity. The Pope actually came to watch the first stone being laid in 1163. The first phase of its completion was around 1270. Then during the Revolution, it came under attack and much of it was destroyed, especially statues from the gallery of kings. The only primary one spared was a 15th-century statue of the Virgin Mary. The church is dedicated to her, after all, or so it is supposed. Finally, in the early 19th century, Notre-Dame was restored and given back to the Catholic Church. It's one of the first of its kind, with vaulted ceilings and massive flying buttresses that seem to defy gravity . . . a true jewel of Gothic art. Suffice it to say that she's had a long and colorful history."

We were at the door, and the familiar sensation of walking from daylight into a dark church returned. Immediately, the smells and sounds swept through my senses, along with feeling the ancient history and significance of one of the greatest churches on Earth. People and tour groups walked about, not so interested in the sacredness of the place, but wanting to take pictures and talk. It made me sad to see how these incredible structures dedicated to prayer and grace are often treated in this modern age. There was no one to demand silence, so it didn't exist.

If only the walls themselves could speak . . . then I remembered—they *were* speaking volumes! Phil had told me that Notre-Dame is really an alchemical text in stone, and the bas-reliefs he pointed out certainly attested to that fact. It felt more like a museum than a church, which seemed to speak to something very deep and forgotten within us.

"Follow me," Phil said as he led me to a back corner of the enormous cavern. "We can do our chanting over here away from most of the people."

The corner did seem to be the safest place, yet we still found that we needed to turn our backs to the open space in order to avoid suspicion. We faced the corner and closed our eyes, taking a few deep breaths. Then, like each time before, we started: *"Elohim Tzabaoth, En Sof; Elohim Tzabaoth, En Sof; Elohim Tzabaoth, En Sof . . ."*

It was as if something in the enormous building took a breath with us as we finished the chant. We both opened our eyes and wondered aloud about our next step. There was a part of me that didn't want to move, wanting instead to hold perfectly still and hope nothing would happen at all. We'd already experienced the strange and the benign, sensing the presence of light and dark angels, as well as more malevolent spirits. Whether any of it was real was still an important question in my mind, although by then, the notion was quickly receding. Something was happening to us and all around us. I still couldn't accurately identify it, but the hours of denial seemed to have passed.

I looked over near the exit and saw an old nun sitting in a chair holding a basket, clearly petitioning donations for whatever charity or convent she was devoted to. She nodded and smiled as people passed her, and the force of her grace alone seemed enough to coax many of them into charitable submission. Although I couldn't be sure, she seemed to look over at me and smile, and it sent a shiver down my spine. Memories of Sacred Heart Basilica returned . . . about the strange man dressed in black who seemed to have been possessed by something in the church, a spirit that seemed to be magnetically drawn to us through the power of the Tetragrammaton.

Was this nun really herself, or was she also inhabited by a wandering, listless ghost that was too afraid to move into the light? Perhaps it couldn't find the light and needed help. I thought of ships that would be lost at sea if not for the blazing beacon of the lighthouse. Maybe this was how the Sacred Names worked: they were the lighthouses that guided lost ships back to safe havens.

I remember Phil telling me that we are all inhabited, even possibly possessed, by what we believe, what we hold to be true. I tried to shake off the feeling as the nun looked back to the line of tourists as they exited. My imagination was getting the best of me, and I knew it. I finally decided to walk around and relax, so I nodded at Phil and started making my way toward the altar.

Until I passed at least three of the cathedral's side altars, I didn't realize that I was actually forcing myself to look straight in front of me, hoping not to be distracted by some metaphysical anomaly that might present itself. It was hard to tell if I'd simply reached my limit for one day, or if there was something drawing me in another direction . . . toward the back of the church it seemed, perhaps to discover the real reason we were there. Whatever the case, I was torn between continuing to walk forward and running in the other direction.

As I reached the main altar, I was amazed by the intricate reliefs sculpted into the long ornate partition that separated the aisle from the tabernacle. Figures of saints and scenes from the life of Jesus stretched along the ancient wood, including the sacred history of the church's most challenged canon and doctrines. Some of the faces in the figures seemed to look out through the wood directly into my soul, and I once again found myself imagining that there was something that was waiting to reach its ethereal hands out to touch my life and deliver a message. I stood there for a moment lingering, even hoping for something to reach out to me—some entities begging me to help them release the heavy grip of whatever formula held them captive. I scanned the wall for several minutes but felt nothing. Whatever promise the cathedral held, it wasn't to be found here.

I continued walking toward the rear of the church, weaving my way through the tourists and groups of sightseers. I came to an altar with a closed iron gate that sheltered a tall statue of St. George with his sword raised to slay the dragon. A crowd of people took glimpses through the gate, looking at the other paintings and statues, but this was the one that drew my attention. St. George had a powerful frame with an athletic build, and the look on his face was determined and unafraid. I was mesmerized by the look in his eyes, and while the crowd filed past from one alcove to the next, I stood there transfixed, unable to even look away. My stare solidified and seemed to lock in place, allowing the saint's face to almost come alive. At this point, I didn't know if it was a real occurrence or the result of my staring. Either way, I didn't seem to have the will to turn and walk away, so I took a deep breath and waited for something to reveal itself.

It was only then that my gaze shifted focus, and I noticed the wall behind the statue. Shields with the Templar cross filled the entire area, framing St. George's raised sword with a powerful energy capable of cutting through any dragon or—how Phil would put it—any remaining vestiges of our Draconian-controlled reptilian brains. When that thought came to mind, I felt a jolt of pain cut through my chest. It pushed me back from the gate at least six inches, and I reached out to steady myself. The pain disappeared but then returned, and for a moment, I thought I was having a heart attack, even though I was sure the intensity had yet to approach that level. Seconds later, it rocketed through me a third time, and I fell to my knees, holding on to the railing to stop my body from hitting the floor. Anyone who stood nearby would have mistaken my movement for sudden religious fervor, but the look on my face would have told a different story. Luckily, the third jolt was the last, but I stayed on my knees in case it returned again.

My heart was racing, and I waited to make sure the incident had finally ended. When I was confident enough to stand, I pulled myself up and leaned against the bars, never taking my eyes away from St. George except to refocus on the Templar crosses behind him. I expected something to happen—a word or phrase spoken out loud or in my mind that would offer me some details or information to explain what was happening . . . but none came. The name we chanted moments earlier did enter my mind, though, so I decided to focus there, reciting the Sacred Name over and over until a new direction revealed itself: *"Elohim Tzabaoth, En Sof; Elohim Tzabaoth, En Sof; Elohim Tzabaoth, En Sof . . ."*

As I chanted, I could feel something building deep within me, starting, it seemed, in my stomach until it reached my chest and then continued into my neck and head. It was a heavy energy, not unpleasant but also not something I wanted to maintain. I kept reciting the name, knowing that the energy I was sensing in the statue was somehow linked to what I was experiencing. Once again, I had the feeling of being caught up in some kind of net or web. The weight seemed to be pulling me back toward the ground, and I thought I was about to fall to my knees again, but as quickly as it began, it ended. I looked at the statue, and it seemed different, although I wasn't sure I could identify how. In my logical mind, I knew it was impossible, but St. George's face seemed more serene and his sword less sharp. I pushed myself away from the gate, almost expecting the pain to return. It didn't, so I stepped back and began walking away.

I walked with a group of Japanese tourists, passing them as they stopped to look at a large painting in another of the side chapels. By then I was nearly at the door, and I saw Phil standing there ready to leave. He smiled, and I gave him a look that told him I was done. It must have revealed more than I'd intended because his smile immediately disappeared and was replaced by a look of concern. I put on my hat as I approached the door and realized just how happy I was to leave Notre-Dame.

A few feet before I reached the exit, I was face-to-face with the nun, and as I passed, she pulled her hands back as if she didn't want anything from me. But her eyes drew me in, and as our gaze met, she smiled and her lips parted.

"Thank you," she said in English. "Thank you."

I paused for no more than a second and then walked out the door.

CHAPTER 13

Heretic Central

El

"What in the world just happened back there?" I asked Phil as we left Notre-Dame Cathedral.

I'd just finished telling him about the statue of St. George and the strange energy I felt, concluding the story with what the nun said to me on the way out of the cathedral. It was as if she were totally aware of what occurred in a part of the church she couldn't see.

"Tell me more about the pain you felt," Phil replied. "You mentioned that you felt it the moment you thought of St. George slaying the dragon."

"Yes, I was thinking about how St. George slew the dragon in the myth, and then I thought about Archangel Michael—a very similar story except that Michael slew Satan, the devil. That's when it hit me."

"That's when what hit you? Was there anything else you saw or felt immediately before the pain started? Did you hear anything?"

"What was strange was the fact that I *didn't* see or hear anything. I know that sounds bizarre, but at this point, the bizarre is normal; it seems odd when unusual things *don't* happen. As soon as I thought the word *devil* and felt the jolt to my heart, I expected that I'd come into contact with some angry spirit that was trapped in that altar. When I realized I hadn't, it made me wonder about the whole thing . . . except that there was no way I made up the pain."

We walked away from the busy square down a street lined with stores and restaurants catering to the millions of tourists who visit every year. The light drizzle we battled most of the day stopped for a short period, and Phil took out his notebook and jotted down a few thoughts as we walked.

"I wish I could tell you what happened in there," he said. "The fact is that unless you can tell me more of what you were thinking or feeling, I can't figure this out any easier than you can. I do know that the parallels between St. George and Michael the Archangel are very strong. Much of what we know of St. George comes to us from the *Golden Legend,* which was brought to us from the Holy Land by means of the Crusades."

"Are you making a connection here with the Templars?"

"Quite possibly. After all, he did protect himself with the sign of the cross. On the other hand, we have Archangel Michael, the Prince of Light, leading the forces of good against the powers of darkness and evil."

"Isn't Michael known as the Good Angel of Death?" I offered.

"Absolutely—and in contrast to Samuel, the Evil Angel of Death. Michael is also known as the field commander of the armies of God, which is why the choice of *Elohim Tzabaoth* at Notre-Dame was inspired, to say the least. He is also known in certain circles as *Sabazios,* or Sky Father. Notice the resemblance to the word *Tzabaoth?* Also, remember that Jews consider Michael an advocate, as strange as that may seem considering the Jewish stance on that kind of intervention. At the same time, some believe that Michael was the teacher of Moses. In the book of Jubilees, Michael is the angel who instructed Moses on the Mount and delivered the tables of the Law to him. Michael called Satan the primitive serpent. Do you now see the connection with George's dragon? This is the true adversary we have to rise above, or slay. The thing about the nun at the exit? That's the most interesting part of the story."

"I agree. What do you think it means?"

"You really felt that her thanking you as we left had to do with what you experienced in the rear of the cathedral, don't you? Do you really think she knew what was happening?"

"I'm almost sure of it!" I was feeling more animated than I'd intended. "She actually pulled her hand back as she said it. I wouldn't have been able to give her any change if I wanted to. And she spoke in English. Do you think she could just tell that I'm not French, or does she speak English to everyone?"

"Well, to be honest, you do look more like the north side of Chicago than Paris. But, seriously, I think what she said was for you—for your ears."

"So do I. I think she knew what was going on or was even a part of it, although I can't imagine how."

"I'm sure how she fits in will be made clear to us as we go on." Phil continued, "I do have a theory, though. I really do feel that Rabbi Eleazar has something to do with all this. Are you familiar with the concept of the *ibbur*?

"Yes, I am. Isn't that when the spirit of a great teacher literally fuses with another person?"

"That's right. The soul of a great sage—in this case, Rabbi Eleazar—bound his spirit to yours, at least for this journey through Paris. This usually happens when more wisdom and faith are called for. And haven't these adventures been a test of your faith and trust, in some form or other? I think what you may have sensed at Notre-Dame, and possibly elsewhere on this journey, was a *dybbuk*, which is an evil or malevolent spirit. In the Jewish folktale called *A Kiss from the Master*, the spirit of the great Kabbalist Shimon bar Yohai comes to someone in a dream. This someone has no experience in the deeper study of the Torah . . . sound familiar? Rabbi Eleazar's soul has braided with yours, in a sense, to help guide us. He came to you in a dream. In a way, he initiated this journey of ours, and I'm just here to dot the i's and cross the t's."

"This is the man who was redeemed even after a lifetime of sin," I added. "Why would he want to help me, especially in something as far out as this adventure?"

"Some of the things you're experiencing have their parallel in his life and teachings. Does that make sense? You were fixated on the statue of St. George who killed the dragon, which could be seen as a symbol of our sinful lower nature or repressive reptilian consciousness. Whatever it was you contacted there, it responded to something within you and the example of Eleazar. Remember, he taught us that there is no sin that cannot be forgiven or soul redeemed.

"I don't think I understand. It all sounds so crazy."

"It may be crazy from one perspective, but we left the sane world behind a long time ago. All I know is that your dream indicated that there's a psychic link, a soul connection between you two. It's an amazing gift. What you're experiencing through this fusion with Eleazar is like a purifying fire, and it's not just for you either. I really believe that everything that's happening to both of us here is for the benefit of so many more—maybe the whole world. And it's the meditation on the Holy Names that has triggered it."

"What about the nun?" I asked.

"I'm guessing that she's so tuned in spiritually that she knew exactly what happened . . . certainly what needed to happen. She was thanking you for what you allowed to occur. Who knows the specifics or what the final effects will be, but you released something very powerful within yourself. She acknowledged it and thanked you."

We walked in silence as we entered the Métro, once more descending into the bowels of Paris. I tried to wrap my mind around not only what just happened, but also Phil's explanation. Even though much of my fear had vanished, I was still apprehensive about our journey. If it really was true that the soul of Rabbi Eleazar had somehow fused with my own and we were sharing the experiences and lessons, then the puzzle pieces were beginning to fall into place. Phil explained that Eleazar wasn't made a rabbi until after he died because his life itself was the teaching, and his name means 'God can help.' He taught us that no one was beyond the healing grace of God.

"Eleazar asked for Divine mercy," Phil recalled. "He asked it of the sun, the moon, the stars . . . especially for Heaven to have mercy on him, but he was told that he has to forgive himself before he can ask for forgiveness from another. A valuable lesson, indeed."

I also thought about the implications this idea had when applied to the modern world. By many accounts, humanity had already passed the point of no return, and some feel that the opportunity to turn the tide back toward a healing path has vanished. If Eleazar's lesson teaches us anything, however, it's that it's never too late. Perhaps humanity is ready to learn the same lesson, and in doing so, begin sustaining rather than destroying the earth.

We exited the Métro at the stop Louvre Rivoli and emerged back into the light. The drizzle had returned, and we stopped for a moment and took in an amazing sight. We were at the east end of the grand Louvre complex, the most famous museum in the world. Within that endless expanse of brick and marble, many of the greatest works of art have found their permanent home, and it didn't surprise me that our adventure would eventually bring us there.

"I had a feeling we'd end up here at some point."

"We're not going to the Louvre," Phil responded. "We're going to a church just across from it: Saint-Germain l'Auxerrois, the Church of the Louvre . . . heretic central."

"Heretic central?"

"Yes. The church used to house an amazing collection of relics, not to mention numerous references, veiled and unveiled, to certain truths the Catholic Church would prefer to keep hidden. I'll tell you more when we're inside." He smirked, which told me that we were in for trouble.

We stopped before we entered, and it seemed that I could emotionally feel something even before we walked inside. Enormous arches marked the entrance, and the stained-glass window at the front of the building promised a grand reward. Phil was quick to point out among the statuary on the exterior of the church the image of Mary Magdalene, with long flowing hair, carrying three loaves of bread. *Heretic central, indeed,* I thought. "Tell me more about this place," I said to Phil.

"Back when the Louvre was still a royal palace, prior to Versailles, Saint-Germain l'Auxerrois was its church. Originally founded in the 7th century, this has been a sacred location for far longer, I assure you. The first major church on this site was built in the early 12th century and was known as Saint-Germain-le-Rond. The church as it stands today is an interesting mixture of Roman, Gothic, and Renaissance styles. The bell tower, which is called *Marie,* is the only element that survives today from the original. What you see here was mainly built in the 13th century. On August 23, 1572, the bells in this tower rang to launch a slaughter of thousands of Protestant Huguenots who had been invited to celebrate the marriage of Henri de Navarre to Marguerite de Valois—now known as the St. Bartholomew's Day Massacre."

"They used the wedding as a way of trapping and murdering thousands of people?"

"Yes, they did," he replied mournfully.

"What a sad place."

"Paris is full of sad places. That's one of the reasons why we're here."

We stepped inside, and I was instantly filled with what could only be described as profound apprehension. I didn't want to be there, but I wasn't sure if it was because of an inherent danger or Phil's story. The knowledge of what happened within the walls centuries earlier was enough to fill me with dread, as if the walls themselves remembered the screams and pain of so many. I closed my eyes so they would quickly adjust to the dim lighting, as well as shutting out the overpowering sensations I felt.

St. Germain was refreshingly devoid of tourists when we arrived. It was easy for us to find a pew in the back and feel like we had the privacy we needed for our ritual. Once we were settled, we began.

Phil opened up his notebook. "The Holy Name we'll chant here is simply *El,* which comes from a root word meaning 'might,' 'strength,' or 'power.' It commonly refers to God, as you know.

When referring to angels or men, it simply means power. It appears 250 times in the Tanakh and around 200 times in the Old Testament. You know, Jimmy, if Moses wanted to get the Old Testament published today, he probably would have to self-publish it. He—"

"Phil, focus."

"Okay, sorry. Among the Canaanites, *El* referred to the Father God. It's often combined with another word, such as *Echad,* producing *El Echad,* meaning 'The One God,' or *El De'ot,* meaning 'God of Knowledge,' as I'm sure you'll recall from our experience at Saint-Roch. You can see from these examples that although it is simple in form, it is profound in its essence. *El* is the key to the Celestial Gate that allows the principle of absolute mercy to flow into the world. *El* is, in fact, the true essence of God. That's why we're going to use it here."

We closed our eyes and began the chant: *"El, En Sof; El, En Sof; El, En Sof . . ."*

Just as we had seven times previously, I felt for the 12 creases of my left knuckles and spoke the sacred words. This name of God echoed off the nearby wall, returning to us like the voices of forgotten souls who once prayed and worshipped there through the centuries. I could feel the energy building as we chanted, and when it was finally over, the silence rose above us as powerfully as the words themselves. We sat for a few more seconds before it was time for me to explore on my own.

"I don't know why, but this place scares me a bit," I confessed. "I think the stories you told me have got me thinking too much."

"You've done this so many times already and nothing truly terrible has happened, has it? Just remember to keep your heart open. You're protected by the name, your faith, and your love. There's nothing here that can harm you."

Phil did his prayer of protection that he'd done at the other locations. I believed what he said, but it didn't do much to relieve the worry and fear that seemed to have overtaken me. I stood up and started walking to the back, as I'd done so many times before in the other churches, hoping I'd stumble upon another welcoming soul like the nun in Notre-Dame. I wasn't too particular about the type of experience I wanted, but my fear was that I'd find an entire assembly of spirits that were lost and unable to leave the place they were slaughtered. I thought about how it might have been to dress up in my finest clothes because I'd received an invitation to attend one of Paris's most anticipated weddings, only to be trapped and butchered because of the particular church I belonged to. The dread I felt seemed to increase as I walked, and by the time I reached the back of the church, I wanted to leave.

Something caught my attention almost immediately, however, that made me want to explore another moment or two. I noticed dozens of Templar crosses decorating the walls that separated the side altars, and there was one altar that seemed to be the primary focus. I walked in and noticed that it was largely bare except for an ancient tabernacle with two doors, both with small Templar crosses on the front. I remembered Phil telling me to always follow the signs, especially when crosses like these show up.

As I approached the altar, I looked up and saw something else that let me know I was in the right place: a beautiful stained-glass window stood just above the tabernacle in four sections. In the center window, Jesus and Mary (as far as I could tell, it was Mary Magdalene) wore crowns of gold and angels were on both sides of them. What made the scene even more interesting was that there were dozens of Yuds—the Hebrew letter that had initiated our journey—adorning the entire scene. The fact that all these signs were in such close proximity to one another confirmed to me that I'd found the source of energy I'd been looking for.

The doors of the tabernacle kept pulling my attention more than anything else I saw. There was a rope to prevent tourists from entering the chapel, but the longer I stood looking, the more I knew I had to break the rule. I looked around to make sure that no one was close enough to see and realized I was completely alone. Then I stepped over the rope and walked the three or four steps until I was directly in front of the altar. My hands were shaking as I reached out, somehow sure that whatever it was I was looking for, the answer was lying behind those doors. I was surprised to find that they weren't locked or even latched. They opened easily, and I leaned forward so I could see inside.

At first, it seemed empty, but the shadow was too deep for me to get a good look. I would have to peer directly inside, perhaps even reach my hand in to feel anything that might be within. The thought sent a wave of fear through my body, enhancing what was already there. Reaching in meant trusting my intuition, but that wouldn't mean anything if my intuition was leading me into danger. I had been skirting along the side of danger since beginning this journey with Phil, and until then, I had done well to avoid it. But this could be pushing the boat to the other shore, and the possibilities both frightened and excited me.

I took a deep breath and slowly stretched out my fingers, reaching as if for a snake whose bite might end my life if caught off guard. My fingers finally broke the empty space left by the open door, then disappeared centimeter by centimeter into the shadowy deep. Soon my entire hand was inside, and I groped about hoping to find something that would justify my breach. My index finger seemed to rub against something rough on the bottom of the tabernacle, perhaps a parchment or piece of cloth, I thought. I tried to wrap my fingers around it to bring it into the light when I heard a loud voice.

"Excusez-moi!" I quickly turned to see a janitor standing a few feet away with a mop held menacingly in his hand. "Que faites-vous?"

I yanked my hand out and starting backing away. "I'm sorry. I was just—"

"Sortez!" He yelled at me to get out.

He rushed toward me as the mop head swung wildly in the air. He was in such a hurry to expel me from the church that he forgot about the rope separating the aisle from the chapel and tripped. Before he was able to regain his balance, though, I was on the other side of him running to the front door.

"Sortez!" he yelled again. Phil heard the commotion and came out of a side chapel just in time to catch sight of us, and I grabbed his arm as I passed.

"Come on—we have to go!" I yelled as we ran. Seconds later, we were out the door jogging down the Place du Louvre. When we were out of sight of the church, we stopped to catch our breath.

"What just happened?" Phil asked me.

"I'd love to tell you, but there's something else I need to do first." I opened my fist to reveal a tiny piece of paper, worn and decayed as if it had been forgotten for decades.

"What is that?"

I told Phil about the tabernacle and the door with the two Templar crosses, and how I reached inside just as the janitor confronted me. "I don't know what it is, but I feel the whole reason we were in that church was to find this." I held out the parchment so we could both see it. There were only two words on it, written in French. "I don't know what it means though."

"I do!" Phil exclaimed. "It says *medal extraordinaire,* which means 'miraculous medal.' I know exactly what it means."

The look in his eyes told me more than words ever could. Miraculous medal? I somehow felt like I was going home.

✧✧✧✧✧

CHAPTER 14

The Incorruptible Saint

Yahweh Tzabaoth

I was 14 years old when Mrs. Meyer gave me the gift that in many ways changed my life. The mother of a friend and classmate of mine, she must have noticed something in me—a bent or inclination toward the mystical side of spirituality, something beyond the rituals and dogma most people cling to in fear. My friend told me about her mother and said that I should come over to the house to meet her. After an hour or so of conversation about saints and other religious topics, she reached out her hand and placed a small object in my palm—a Miraculous Medal.

"I think my parents gave me one when I was confirmed a few years ago," I told her. "I never really understood what it meant, though."

"It's sign of devotion to the Blessed Mother," she replied. "Every great saint was devoted to her, and if you're going to follow their example, you should do the same."

"You think I'm meant to follow the example of saints?" I asked in disbelief. The idea seemed so foreign and unreachable that I didn't even want to consider it.

She was smiling. "I don't think you're going to follow their example. I think you're going to be an example—and if you choose to, you could be a saint yourself. I can see it in your eyes, the fidelity and the devotion. But you're going to need her help if you want to stay pure. The medal will help you. It's a way of giving yourself to her care, and once you're hers, she never lets you go. Just keep the medal close, and everything will work out on its own."

I never forgot that conversation. Within seconds, it was attached to a chain I wore around my neck and was with me for years. Unfortunately, somewhere along the way, I lost it, as well as the original enthusiasm that Mrs. Meyer helped inspire. But it was still there, deep in the back of my mind. All it took was a little prodding, and perhaps an ancient-looking piece of parchment.

✡✡✡

"That piece of paper you found changes everything," Phil said, pulling me out of my reverie, as we walked toward the Métro.

"It does? What does it change?"

"First of all, it changes where we're going to next. I chose ten places to visit according to their importance and my intuitive guidance. I actually had something completely different in mind for the ninth location; however, you finding this piece of paper tells me that we're meant to go somewhere else, a place I'd originally chosen but then changed my mind about."

"Where is it?"

"Before I reveal that, there's something else I need to tell you. Don't you think it's strange that so many symbols and clues were present at St. Germain? It tells me that we were meant to find that parchment. The only question is who put it there? And why? Was it there for us to find, to guide us to our next location? I told you that there were allies assisting us on this journey. The parchment is very old, but there's really no way to tell. And the words *medal extraordinaire*. As far as I know, they only mean one thing, and that's why we have to change our route."

"Change our route?"

"Have you ever hear of the Miraculous Medal?"

"Of course I have. Every Catholic knows about it. They used to hand them out like candy."

"How much do you know about its history or where it came from?"

"I used to know a bit, but it's been awhile." Phil and I were standing on the platform waiting for the train. It was late in the afternoon by then, and the Métro was busier than it had been earlier, so we moved to the far side where it was less crowded.

"There was a nun here in Paris named Catherine Labouré from the Daughters of Charity. One night in 1830 she woke up to the sound of a young child asking her to come to what's called the 'Sister's Chapel.' The place where it happened is very near here. The Blessed Mother Mary appeared to Catherine that night and said she was going to charge her with a special mission. Later that year, Catherine had another vision of Mary standing inside an oval shape on a globe. She also saw the following in a halo around her head: 'O Mary conceived without sin, pray for us who have recourse to thee.' Mary then instructed her to have a medal made depicting what she saw, telling her that those who wear it would receive great grace. At first it was known as the 'Medal of the Immaculate Conception' but was later changed to the 'Miraculous Medal.'"

"Yes, that all sounds familiar."

"But do you know what happened to Catherine after her experience?" Phil asked.

"I don't think so. What?"

"No one other than her confessor actually knew that she was the one who brought the Miraculous Medal to the world. She spent most of her life as an ordinary nursing sister, and she died in 1876. In 1933, her body was exhumed and was discovered not to have decayed."

"Yes, I remember now. She's one of the incorruptibles. There are many saints throughout Europe who are on display in various churches and cathedrals whose bodies have not decayed."

"That's correct. As for Catherine, almost 60 years had passed, and it looked like she'd just died. It was considered a miracle, one of the graces that Mary said she would bestow. Since then, Catherine rests in a glass coffin at the side altar in a church at 140 rue du Bac, inside the chapel at the Mother House where the Blessed Mother appeared. As I've said, it wasn't one of the places on my list, but given the discovery you just made, I now feel it should be. We're going to the Chapel of Our Lady of the Miraculous Medal."

I looked down at the piece of paper in my hand. Was it really meant to guide us to the church where a saint's incorrupt body now lay? If so, what was the connection? The train pulled into the station as I was contemplating this, and we stepped into the already overflowing car. Phil was pushed in one direction and I was pushed in the other, and we held on to the steel pole as it jerked forward, pulling us closer to the next step. But what was it a step toward? It was the first time I'd asked myself that question, suddenly needing a purpose that would offer some deeper meaning to all of these experiences. Each spot we visited and the Sacred Names we chanted gave me a deeper appreciation of the power in the names themselves. But there had to be a deeper reason for it all, and the piece of paper I found was a step toward its revelation.

I thought about Mrs. Meyer and the Miraculous Medal she gave me. It was a gift and a step that led to so many other openings and opportunities—all of which led to that moment in Paris, bumping along on the Métro. Within days after speaking with my friend's mom, my life completely changed. My prayers and devotions took on a new level of dedication, and my heart seemed to open to a deeper intimacy with the Divine, a shift that has driven my life ever since. Through Mrs. Meyer, I discovered a sacred wealth of fidelity and grace that had eluded me until then. My spiritual life went from fulfilling my Sunday obligation to attending daily mass and praying my rosary each morning before school. It was a juvenile beginning, but one that gained profound momentum as I grew up.

Years later when I felt the desire to expand my journey to include more than the narrow frame I had been raised with, that devotion never left me. And I couldn't relate to those I met who felt wounded by their upbringing, calling themselves 'recovering Catholics.' For me, my faith was a continued source of strength, like a beloved mother who may live in a different state but continues to exert tremendous influence.

We stopped at Saint-Placide and filed off the train. When we reached the street, I noticed that we were in a trendy neighborhood with designer clothing stores and upscale food markets serving its chic clientele. We walked several blocks and turned down rue du Bac, and in the distance, I could see people standing outside a large churchlike building. Near the alley that led between two buildings stood a young bearded Franciscan, and I recognized him as being part of a burgeoning community from the Bronx in New York called the Franciscan Order of Atonement.

I'd read about the order in several magazines commenting on their back-to-basics approach to religious life. His beard was at least five inches long, leading me to believe (if it were true that members were forbidden to shave their facial hair) that this man had been a member of the community for several years. His presence lent an air of conservatism to a shrine that I knew attracted more traditional Catholics, a group I was for the most part raised and rooted in. Memories were streaming into my mind as we approached the building, and I held the parchment in my left hand as if someone were going to steal it from me at any moment.

We turned left into the entrance that was still open to the air and rain, walking toward the door at the end of the alley where the real action surely awaited us. A door to the right led to a small bookstore where older nuns, clearly the descendants of their Sister Catherine, sold large bags filled with medals to be passed out to members of churches or prayer groups when the tourists returned home.

"It's funny that fate brought us here," Phil remarked. "When I was researching and trying to decide where we would go, this church was an original choice, but like I said, I'd changed my mind."

"Why did you change your mind?"

"I'm not really sure," he said as we stopped in front of the doors that led into the main church. "It just didn't add up at the time, but now it makes perfect sense."

It was unusual at first to walk into a chapel that was so much smaller than the other churches we'd visited. A brilliant light seemed to radiate from the altar, and although the lamps that illumined the central statue of Mary were perhaps brighter than they needed to be, I sensed that there was something more, something I couldn't see with my eyes that inspired a sense of awe. Above the altar, a wondrous tableau commemorating Catherine's apparitions with Mary drew the attention of every person there, and the angels that surrounded them seemed to have a quality that made them seem real, although I knew it was impossible. The statue of Mary was meant to resemble Catherine's vision: the glowing halo, a circle of 12 stars, and outstretched arms. As always, stone angels surrounded her, sentinels holding sacred space and guarding the bridge that separated Heaven and Earth.

Then I saw something that confused me at first. To each side of the main altar, two glass coffins rested on the ground, each seeming to contain the remains of a nun. Phil had mentioned only one incorruptible, Catherine, but there seemed to be an additional saint resting in front of us. I turned to him, and he seemed to recognize my puzzlement.

"I don't know," he replied. "I didn't know of any other incorruptibles here. Let's go to the front and see if it says anything there."

We crossed to the far aisle, and I found myself instinctively genuflecting when I passed in front of the tabernacle holding the Blessed Sacrament—a custom I'd learned and practiced from the time I was a child but which I thought had been abandoned. I made the sign of the cross, then stood again to follow Phil. He looked back at me and smiled, probably wondering why I suddenly chose to follow the custom there but not in any of the other Catholic churches we'd visited. I shrugged my shoulders as if to say that I didn't have an answer either, for him or for myself.

In some ways, this church reminded me of the devotions that had been so important to me when I was young, but as I grew older, praying the rosary or wearing the Miraculous Medal became less important. At that time, the church was my entire spiritual world, and it wasn't until I left college that I'd discovered a new world where I could apply the same lessons to a wide variety of expressions. Years later I would put the peace prayers from the 12 major religions of the world to music, and in doing so, my reach expanded to uncovering the essence of peace found in every spiritual path. But when I came to places like this—churches where the old practices were still honored and devotion to the Blessed Mother was still in vogue—something dormant within me came to life, and I found myself automatically returning to the practices of my youth.

We made our way to the glass coffin sitting to the left of the altar that contained the body of a nun in an ancient habit. Beneath the container, there was an inscription that revealed her identity.

"Saint Louise de Marillac," Phil read in a soft voice. A bright mosaic rose above her with two angels in prayer looking down upon the body, and a dove symbolizing the Holy Spirit shining its light onto the middle of the casket. "I think she was the founder of the order."

"One of the founders," a voice behind us corrected him in a thick French accent. We turned around to see a small nun, perhaps in her 70s, smiling up at us. "She helped St. Vincent de Paul found the order. Oh, hers was an amazing story."

"Can you tell us more about her?" I asked in as soft a voice as possible.

"Well, she was born in 1591, and she was illegitimate, which meant she was despised by so many. She wanted to be a nun, but instead she married and had a son named Michel. When her husband died, she decided to give her life in service to others, and this is when she met St. Vincent. They would visit the poor together, and she ultimately became his collaborator in starting the order. She was very holy, and that is why she is here near the altar."

"But sister," Phil said, "I didn't realize there was more than one incorruptible here. I thought that St. Catherine was the only one."

"She is. This isn't the real St. Louise; it's just a wax image of her. St. Catherine is the only one whose body has withstood the ravages of time."

We were both surprised by this. The body beneath the glass seemed so real and natural. It was easy to believe that the miracle had happened twice.

"What does it mean?" I asked her. "There must be a reason why St. Catherine's body didn't decay as normal."

"There is a reason," she said. "It's grace. The grace of Our Lady filled her completely as a reward for her humility and service. Catherine was the perfect example of everything Mary expressed. She didn't draw attention to herself but to the beauty and holiness that was demonstrated to her. Even though she died, her body remained whole, and her soul remained free. Come, I want to show you something."

We walked with her as she crossed in front of the altar, genuflected, and then walked to the body of St. Catherine. I followed her example and genuflected as I passed and Phil did the same. Then we stopped directly in front of the glass coffin. Catherine was dressed in the same style of habit as when she was buried, although there was no way for me to know if it was the exact same one. I assumed it was since it had been either encased here at the altar or beneath the ground held separate from the elements.

"Come close so we can speak softly," she whispered. We moved in as she pointed toward the body. "Everything looks perfectly normal, but there is one thing you could say is unusual. Tell me if you can see what it is."

I looked at the body beneath the glass and had a difficult time determining what *wasn't* unusual. Her wimple seemed as clean and starched as the day she was first professed, and the famous symbol that could be found on all Miraculous Medals was embossed in gold behind her midsection. In her hands, which pointed straight upward, were the beads of a black rosary balanced between her fingers as if she were still deep in prayer. As much as we looked, though, neither one of us could spot anything obviously out of place.

"Don't look for what is missing," the nun instructed, "but for what is there in abundance."

I tried to follow the train of her words, but as long as I looked, nothing seemed abnormal, given, of course, the strange circumstances we were dealing with.

Finally, Phil spoke up. "The rosary. She has two rosaries, one in the hand and one at her side."

I looked and realized that he was correct. There was a second rosary lying at her side, as was customary for a nun's habit, in addition to the one in her hands.

"That's right," she affirmed. "Very good. Now, as soon as you discover why she has two rosaries, then you'll solve the mystery."

"The mystery?" I asked, as if she'd read our minds. "What mystery?"

"The mystery of the medal and of St. Catherine's incorruptible body. They're linked, you know. Understand one and you'll understand them both." She walked away smiling, toward the back of the church. I looked at Phil.

"Was it a coincidence that she spoke of a mystery involving the medal?"

"There are no accidents," he replied, gazing through the glass at her pale and lifelike body. "We were led here because of a tiny parchment that said *medal extraordinaire*. Now we're told there's a mystery around the two rosaries. Why? It isn't just a coincidence, that's for sure."

"Any idea what it means then?"

Phil didn't say anything for several seconds but stood looking at every detail of the body, the rosary, even the clothing she wore. His eyes consumed every detail like a fire moving over the scene, and I wondered if he perceived something that was invisible to me. Then he took a deep breath and relaxed. "No, I don't know what it means. Not yet. But I do believe that we were led here and that it's all part of the puzzle. I suggest we sit down and chant the next name. Every other time it has initiated something, like a chain reaction, that brought us to the right spot or the perfect experience. I'm sure the same thing will happen here."

"But this isn't like the other places we've visited," I added. "This isn't a Gothic cathedral that was built with the Templar symbols and ancient formulas etched in the walls. This is a relatively new church, so I can't imagine that it has the same charge the others had."

"You may be right, but there's something here—at the very least, there's something for us to learn. When we were in Saint-Germain l'Auxerrois, you were led to the side chapel where you saw the tabernacle with the Templar crosses, right?"

"Yes, that's correct."

"And the tabernacle just happened to be open, and there just happened to be this piece of paper with the words *medal extraordinaire*. It seems too convenient, too easy, don't you think?"

"I didn't question it till now . . . but maybe. What does it mean?"

"It almost makes me feel like it was put there for us, but by whom?"

"Who would have put it there?" I asked in disbelief. "No one knows we're here, and even if they did, how could they have known that I would look there?"

"Don't be so naïve. It's no secret we're here. We haven't been alone since we started this journey. We've been making ourselves known in some pretty dramatic ways, and not only to other people."

"Now you're scaring me."

"I didn't necessarily mean that the way it sounded." Phil took me by the arm and walked me to the side. Two older women were trying to get closer to Catherine's body, and I had the sense we were starting to speak over a whisper. "What I meant to imply is that we're not alone. Maybe that's what the parchment was about. Maybe it was meant to remind us that we're doing important work here, and that we should keep going."

"Why all the mystery, then? First the paper, then the nun. What did she say about the rosaries?"

"She said that if we could figure out why there were two rosaries, we would understand why Catherine's body remained uncorrupted. And I think I have the answer—at least part of it." He moved a foot or so to the left so we could see into the glass coffin where Catherine lay. "One rosary is at her side, but pay attention to the one in her hands. Maybe it's not so much about the rosary itself but the hands that hold it. Notice that her hands are turned upward, in prayer position. Her fingers are pointing straight up, almost as if they're pointing to something. Do you see that?"

I realized that Phil was onto something. Her fingers indeed seemed to be pointing, but toward what? I looked above the glass coffin and saw a brilliant white statue of the Blessed Mother directly above her, a direct line from her upturned fingers. I took a step closer to see if there was anything in the statue that might give another clue, a symbol or a familiar sign. None seemed obvious, though I couldn't let go of the feeling that there was something I wasn't picking up on.

"Let's go back over to the side," Phil said as he pulled me into a pew. "It's time for us to do the chant. I'm sure something more will happen once we focus on the name I've chosen."

"What name is that?"

"The Sacred Name we'll be using here is *Yahweh Tzabaoth*, which means 'Lord of Hosts.'"

I noticed we were going to repeat what we chanted at our first stop. "We're back to the Tetragrammaton. Are you going to vocalize something else again like we did at Sacred Heart?"

"No. This time we're going to actually stay with *Yahweh* and simply add the word *Tzabaoth*."

"Wait a minute. You gave me this whole speech about how the Most Holy Name can't be vocalized. This is really confusing. Which is it?"

"Do what you feel is right. Let's allow Spirit to move us since this place is so different than the others. We're in a spot where a miracle occurred a little over a hundred years ago. The other locations we've visited are older and have much more history. I was going to recommend using a different word than *Yahweh* just as we did before, but I feel like I'm following something here. I say we go with it."

"Hey, I'm not the one who had an issue with it in the first place, and I don't have an issue with it now," I added. "I don't feel quite ready, though. Do you mind if I walk around a bit more?"

"I was actually going to suggest that we move about the church a bit more and let the perfect place find us. There's an incredible amount of energy in this church, and it seems to be moving us effortlessly into a very deep experience. We can begin our chant once we've located the spot we need to be in."

I could sense the strong energy all around me, as if I were being enveloped in a feeling of grace that I'd never experienced before. My first instinct was to walk back to St. Catherine's body and look for more clues, but when I stepped into the aisle, I felt a strange sensation, almost like I was being pulled backward. I decided not to resist the urge and found myself walking to the rear of the church. It was a subtle feeling but one I couldn't ignore. I walked to the back and stood by the door, stepping to the side as people walked in and out of the entrance. From that spot, I had a clear view of the altar and the two coffins, one with the body of St. Catherine and the other with the wax effigy of St. Louise.

As I stood there, an idea seemed to enter my mind that I didn't expect. I suddenly remembered the obelisk and the stereogrammatic vision Phil taught me. I wasn't sure why, but I had the feeling to look in the direction of Catherine and the statue of Mary with this form of soft focus, letting my eyes slightly cross and fade in and out. I hoped no one was looking because it must have appeared very strange. A minute or two passed as I followed my guidance, and it was only when I decided that it was pointless that I saw something out of the ordinary.

In the statue above St. Catherine, Mary held a golden globe with a thin cross at the very top. I had the sensation that the globe began to move, almost lift from her hands, and I closed my eyes for a second to see if it was really happening. When I opened them again, everything had returned to normal, but after a few seconds, the globe once again seemed to lift a few inches from her hands. And as I retained a soft focus, it appeared to keep lifting and then fell slowly toward the glass coffin. I watched and held my gaze, and it continued to fall until it seemed to come to rest at the tip of Catherine's fingers. I blinked, but the vision remained. I didn't want to look away because I was convinced that there was a message for me, as if I was seeing something that wasn't really there for anyone else, and it had great significance.

Then I heard a quiet feminine voice enter my mind. At first it was like a whisper, but the single phrase seemed to gain momentum until it penetrated my entire being.

"Pray for the whole world. Pray for the whole world."

Was it *her* voice—Mary, the mother of Jesus? The sound made me feel buoyant, and my soul felt like it was lifting from my body, just as the globe lifted from her hands.

"Use the name and pray for the whole world." By now an ecstatic feeling rushed through me, and I thought I might actually lose consciousness. I was barely aware of Phil as he touched my arm, bringing me back just enough to hear what he said.

"I don't know what you're experiencing, but I believe it's time for us to use the name I've chosen for this location."

I nodded my head, which is all I seemed capable of at the moment, and we began: *"Yahweh Tzabaoth, En Sof; Yahweh Tzabaoth, En Sof; Yahweh Tzabaoth, En Sof . . ."*

It felt like a key was being inserted into the proper hole, and all the tumblers were suddenly falling into place. I'm not sure how, but the Sacred Name seemed to trigger something in the globe that was still floating near the tip of Catherine's fingers. It was beginning to glow and radiate a golden silvery light that soon encompassed and surrounded her entire body. It seemed to be enveloping her—that's the only way I can describe it—as if the energy was holding her in a state of suspended animation. Was I actually witnessing the miracle of her incorruptibility? Was this why her skin was as intact as it was the day she died 120 years earlier?

Behind her in the casket, the medal she was famous for reflected the light of the radiating globe, and in that instant, I knew why we were drawn there. It was impossible to know if someone had placed the parchment in the last church for us to find, or if they were simply meaningless words with no connection to what we were now experiencing. Coincidence or not, they drew us to this spot, to the church where a marvelous miracle was taking place. Holiness and grace were flowing from Heaven through this statue, imbuing the body of this faithful nun with an unearthly energy that could defy the laws of time. It was indeed a *medal extraordinaire,* and through the Holy Name, I was blessed to directly perceive it.

"It's so beautiful," I murmured just below my breath.

"I didn't hear you," Phil whispered. "What was it?"

But as much as I wanted to tell him, I couldn't speak. All I could do was hold on to the ecstasy and grace that was by then filling me completely. Tears were flowing down my cheeks, and I barely sensed the presence of the helpful nun who spoke to us at the front of the church earlier.

She looked at me and smiled. "Maintenant vous comprenez . . . now you understand. It's nice when someone understands what's happening here."

CHAPTER 15

Chartres Cathedral

Ehyeh Asher Ehyeh

We arrived back at our apartment early in the evening, and there was only one thing I wanted to do: sit perfectly still and not think about the events of that perplexing day. As we walked up the stairs, we passed the bizarre painting of Rhett Butler and Scarlett O'Hara, as well as the ghastly portraits of demons and men enduring horrendous torture. *Just what I needed,* I thought to myself. It had been a day of slow torment mixed with moments of sheer ecstasy—and now I was back in a place that seemed more like hell's waiting room than a bed-and-breakfast.

"What should we do tonight?" Phil asked, as if I had any interest at all in a nighttime excursion. "How about Moulin Rouge? That would be amazing after everything we saw today."

"I think I'd rather have toothpicks inserted through my eyelids," I blurted out, as I fell onto the couch. "You do what you want, but I'm not going anywhere. Just knowing there's still one place left on our Kabbalah tour of Paris makes me feel even more exhausted. Why won't you tell me where we're going tomorrow?"

"I wanted it to be a surprise—the cherry on top of the sundae!" he exclaimed with far more enthusiasm than I could bear.

"I think I've had enough surprises. If there's no esoteric reason for not revealing it, I hope you'll take me out of my misery and spill it now."

"Fine." Phil sat down across from me in a large stuffed chair. "We're going to one of the most amazing churches in the world—Chartres Cathedral. You've probably heard of the famous Chartres labyrinth, as well as some important relics we'll find there that I'm sure might be of special interest to you."

I sat up straight in my chair. "Of course! I've always wanted to go to Chartres. That's great news . . . but it's not in Paris. How far away is it?"

"It's 80 kilometers from Paris—a very easy trip. I figured we can get some breakfast and spend a good part of the day there. That's the benefit of having accomplished so much today. Now we don't have to rush."

"What can you tell me about the cathedral?" I asked.

"Well, first of all, the proper name is the Cathedral of Our Lady of Chartres, or Cathédrale Notre-Dame d'Chartres. It was built in honor of Mary, mother of Jesus, and is sometimes called the 'Seat of the Virgin Mary on Earth.' Even before it was built, it was a very important Marian pilgrimage destination with enormous fairs that honored Mary with many feasts dedicated to her."

"That's always a distinction we need to make in France: Mary Magdalene always seems to creep in somewhere."

"Mary Magdalene will always insinuate herself, especially in this part of the world, either overtly or covertly. Worship of the Magdalene has often been replaced by the Blessed Mother since the Catholic Church has always had an uneasy relationship with *the other Mary*. Anyway, because of its history, it was only natural that in the year 876, it became the home of the tunic of Our Lady, called the *Sancta Camisia*. It was supposedly given to the cathedral by Charlemagne who received it as a gift during a crusade in Jerusalem. None of that's true though . . . you know how legends go. It was actually presented by a man named Charles the Bald, and it's believed that the fabric came from Syria. Carbon dating proves that it was woven in the 1st century. It's all very interesting, don't you think?"

"I think it's interesting that his name was Charles the Bald," I added as I reached up and rubbed my own head.

"I thought you might like that. And here's something even more interesting: in 1194, there was a fire in the church that nearly destroyed everything. The townspeople, as you might imagine, went completely crazy. It didn't seem possible for Mary's tunic to have survived. It was one of the most crucial relics in Christendom, and it was gone. What they didn't know was that some of the priests hid with it in an underground vault (in the crypt that we'll be visiting tomorrow) that was beneath the main church. Three days later, after everything cooled down, they emerged carrying the relic. Can you imagine what that must have been like? The entire town is mourning the loss of their most precious possession, and three days later, the priests walk out through the smoke and debris carrying it high in the air."

"So it's still there . . . the tunic?"

"Yes, of course: the tunic, the crypt, Our Lady of the Pillar, and even Chartres's Black Madonna. That's why we're going tomorrow—all those reasons and more, as you'll soon find out."

I stood up from the couch and began pacing the room. "Do you see how significant this is? We were led to the Chapel of Our Lady of the Miraculous Medal by a seeming coincidence, and it was while we were there that I actually believe I saw how Mary was keeping St. Catherine's body intact. Now we're going to the cathedral that houses her actual tunic. That can't be a simple coincidence. I have the feeling that a great part of this journey is being guided by her, in one way or another. Does that make any sense?"

"I can't say for sure," Phil replied, "but it does seem possible. We've been using various Kabbalistic-related names of God to unlock the keys to our own souls, knowing that we would be helping to release other forms of sentient consciousness in the places we've been visiting, both physical and nonphysical. Somehow she keeps showing up in the equation."

"Mary has always been believed to be the perfect reflection of God's grace, much like the moon reflects the sun. So it stands to reason that she's been behind much of this journey."

"I think you might be right."

"What about the name?" I inquired. "There's one in particular that seems to have been missing."

"I figured you would notice. You used it as the foundation of the Moses Code: *Ehyeh Asher Ehyeh,* 'I AM THAT, I AM.' I've been saving it for Chartres because I knew it would have the most impact, although I don't think I realized just how much until now. Everything we've experienced seems to have led us to this point, straight back to the Mother."

"That's somewhere I'm very comfortable," I remarked.

"What do you mean?"

"I don't know how much I've ever told you about this, but my entire youth was spent praying my rosary, wearing my Miraculous Medal, and giving myself to Mother Mary. It's the reason I decided to join the Franciscans when I was 18. I may have gone off in other directions since then, but my devotion to Mary has always been a center point of my spirituality."

"That's great to hear," Phil said, "and you may want to hold on to that because the way this day has gone, there's no telling what will happen next."

✡✡✡

I was back in Jerusalem, but everything looked different from what I remembered. People walked through the street speaking to one another and holding hands, and the smell of incense filled the air. It took me several seconds to recall my previous visit with Rabbi Eleazar, when I sat in the café and learned more about the mission that Phil and I were about to embark on. Since that conversation, we had experienced so much, more than I could have ever imagined. I hoped that I'd find him there again and that he'd be able to tell me more about our last day in Paris, and what it all meant.

As I walked, I noticed a woman who sat staring straight ahead with a young boy on her lap. It struck me as strange, and as I watched, the boy sprung from her lap and grabbed my hand, pulling me through the crowd of people, darting around them as we passed. It was only then that I realized he was the same boy from my dream the night before—the one who led me to the pregnant woman—although he seemed perhaps younger now. When we finally stopped, I noticed that we were back at the café where I had my conversation with Eleazar. The boy let go of my hand and climbed onto the lap of another woman with dark olive skin, different from the one I saw him with before, yet she too sat silently, staring straight ahead. Then I heard a familiar voice speaking.

"Come and sit down, my son. You do know where you are, yes?"

I turned and saw Eleazar sitting at a table. It was similar to the one we sat at the last time we met, but it was also higher, and I noticed that the tablecloth was much more colorful. I walked over to him and sat down.

"I'm back in Jerusalem, aren't I? Isn't this the same place we met last night?"

"Look around and tell me what you see." He waved his huge hands in the air as he said these words, and it was only then that I noticed that things were indeed very much different. People walked around us in modern dress; and I saw merchants' tables filled with jeans, cell phones, CDs, and pirated DVDs.

"It's Jerusalem," I replied, "but it's now modern-day Jerusalem, not ancient times like it was last night."

"Last week or 2,000 years ago . . . time means little in this world." Eleazar sipped his tea. "It is the same place, but everything is different as you can see. But you are the same, and I am the same. And that means that God is the same. Do you understand?"

"Yes, I think I do. Times and places may vary from one era to another, but truth and God are constant. They don't shift from one period to another."

Eleazar nodded and smiled. "Very good. And what about this music . . . it would make anyone *meshuga*. The sacred music of my time fills one with a sense of longing: the longing of the soul's vessel for the light and the longing to return to the state of Devekut, which is the state of spiritual union with the Creator."

It was only then that I heard the sound of rap music blaring from a nearby window. Eleazar plugged his ears and smiled, making a larger demonstration than he needed to.

"I can see what you mean," I said to him, "but will you tell me more about the soul's longing for the light?"

"As you ask, my son. It is from the teaching of the Beloved Ari, blessed be he. He spoke of the original vessels that were not able to contain the sheer power of the spiritual light that was poured into them. As a result, they shattered. The vessels were made to be able to hold or contain the light, but they were no longer able to. Before the beginning, everything was filled with the light of *En Sof.*"

"Is this what happens when we receive more light than we can handle?" I asked. "This seems to be what many people are experiencing at this time on our planet."

"This is very important, and I want you to try to understand." Eleazar leaned over the table and moved a foot closer, staring into my eyes with an intensity I hadn't ever experienced. "When that happens, when the soul is no longer able to contain the light, there is a restriction, but this restriction allows a new creation to occur. It is related to the concept of what's called *Tzimtzum,* whereby a void was created into which the *Light of Existence* is poured. The question is: Are you ready to make room in your life—in your heart—for your new creation? This, as you'll soon see, is what your journey has been all about."

"Yes, rabbi, I believe I am. This is why we're here, and why I'm sitting with you now."

"Yes, but first the curtains or the veils that hide the light need to be removed."

"Is that what Phil and I have been doing with the names?"

"You've been using the Sacred Names to connect with the ongoing moment of creation," he answered, leaning back in his seat again. "The names are mathematical programs. Think of it in this way: when you need to access information in those things that have been invented that do so many things and are so powerful—"

"Do you mean our computers?"

"Yes, that's exactly what I mean. When you need information from your computer, there is something you need first. Do you know what it is? It allows you to begin."

"Yes," I answered, "we need a password or a pass code."

"Precisely. And these are what the names are: they're passwords. They are keys that unlock gates of light within you—celestial gates. They open your heart and allow your light to shine. They allow access to the most secret chambers of the heart: to the intelligence of the heart. They will open to your future and your past, allowing them to fuse into the present moment."

"And when we finally open our hearts in this way, what will we find?"

"What will you find? Ah, that's the big question, isn't it? All I can tell you is that this is a very special moment, my son. Now is the time for the repair of the world, the *Tikkun Olam*. Even to nonmystical Jews, the concept of *Tikkum Halev* points to a restoration of the human heart and soul to a primordial state of unity and harmony that was known and experienced before what's called the 'Shattering of the Vessels.' We are all Holy Sparks longing to return to the state of unity we knew before the creation of the world, before the fall. The Creation, your world, is in a damaged state right now, a state of imperfection, and special souls have come at this time of correction to restore and reinvigorate humanity."

"I feel that there's a very special role for the Divine Feminine in all this," I added. "The role of Mary seems to be coming up again and again in this journey, both Mary the Mother of Jesus and Mary Magdalene. Am I on the right track with this? Is this all about the Divine Feminine finally bringing balance to the world?"

"You are closer than you know," he said smiling. "It is she who will crush the serpent's head—the serpent being the egoic world that seems to reign. She is the Shekinah returning from her exile. When she does, then all shadows will disappear, and a new world crowned in glory will rise. Do you know what I'm referring to?"

Instantly a scene from the book of Revelation popped into my mind: the apocalypse of St. John, of a woman with the sun and moon at her feet and a crown of 12 stars around her head holding the child—the son who would rule the world to come. "Yes, I think I do. It's one of the signs of the end times. Is that what you're saying—that she signals the end of the world?"

"All I'll say for now is that you are very close," Eleazar replied. "Continue following the signs, and let the Sacred Names guide your way. You'll soon discover that this goes far deeper than you realize. There is still a Torah invisible to human eyes. It will show you how beginning and ending are to be joined."

✡✡✡

I woke up to the sound of music in the next room—what seemed like some kind of jazz-rock fusion, far more than I hoped to hear so early in the morning. I looked at the clock: 7:30. The desire to go back to sleep escaped me, and I assumed this was Phil's way of getting the day moving. I threw my legs over the side of the bed and made my way to the bathroom.

"What do you think?" he asked as I entered the living room moments later. "I found a few CDs. Nice way to get the blood going when you're in Paris!" He looked so happy and excited about the final day of our adventure. I didn't feel that I could share his enthusiasm until after a strong cup of coffee and perhaps even a visit to our favorite crepe shop.

"It's a bit much for me right now. Maybe just a tad softer?"

Phil turned the CD player off. "Just didn't want you to sleep too long with Chartres waiting for us. I have a good feeling about this final leg. How are you feeling?"

I wondered if I should tell Phil about the most recent dream with Eleazar. I decided to hold off and see where things led. So much had already transpired, and I knew that everything would work out just as it was meant to, regardless of my interference. "I'm feeling like moving along and getting on the train," I told him. "Did you check the schedule?"

"The train leaves every hour from Gare Montparnasse, so we're fine. I do agree that there's no time to waste, though. Everything's about to fall into place, and I for one am curious about what that will look like."

✡✡✡

The train rolled through the French countryside, and the sun began elbowing its way through the dark clouds. It was a pleasant relief to know we wouldn't have to struggle through the rain again as we had the previous day; the elements were finally on our side. Perhaps it was a sign of things to come: that we were about to enjoy a whole new range of possibilities and learn how the various names of God fit together in some kind of coherent whole.

That was the truth of it—regardless of what it's called, God is one and we are one in God. We'd wrestled with and been blessed by the various energies we encountered along the way, but in the end, they all led back to the same place . . . *me*. I realized that it wasn't a personalized "me" I felt, but the truth within each one of us. Whoever we are and whatever we experience, God's grace is personal and intimately involved in our lives. The journey we had chosen was a journey to the core of who we really are—Phil, me, and each one of us. The lesson may be simple when approached through the mind, but when claimed by the heart, it's an experience that can change the world.

The train turned a corner, and I could see a village in the distance. In the center of the village, two enormous spires rose above the roofs and trees, giving the impression of angel wings spreading over all the inhabitants of Chartres. For more than a thousand years, the cathedral watched silently as the rest of the town grew and matured. It alone remained the same, expressing a constancy that's refreshing and rare in these modern times.

"The cathedral is a short walk from the train," Phil said as we approached the station. "I say we make our way there and begin right away. If there's still time at the end, we can explore a bit."

"What do you expect here?" I asked, hoping for at least a guess.

"There's no telling," he replied, without looking away from the window of the train. "Yesterday we helped open energy channels and portals within us and within these structures that have been resting or blocked for centuries. That's bound to have an impact in ways we can't begin to imagine. I don't mean to be mysterious or evasive, but it all comes down to Chartres, and to the name *Ehyeh*

Asher Ehyeh. Tell me what you've learned about that particular Sacred Name."

I was surprised by the question, especially since we were seconds away from arriving in the village of Chartres. *There must be some significance,* I thought, so I looked inward and spoke more from my heart than from my mind. "Moses asked one of the most important questions in history. He asked God for a name, but not just *any* name. The name God gave helped Moses understand the nature of Divine Presence. The Israelites didn't have a name for God at that point, other than appellations that represented qualities or attributes or even terms of reverence. God was always at arms length, separate and somewhere in the distance.

"Moses realized that *Ehyeh Asher Ehyeh* (I AM THAT, I AM) offered the key for creating miracles, not only in their lives but for the entire world. Moses claimed the freedom that the Israelites desperately sought, and with the Holy Name of God on his lips, there was nothing that could stop him. It's a lesson that has been overlooked for 3,500 years, but now I think it's time for all of us to realize that we're no different than Moses—that we have the power within us to create miracles. The name of God is our name, in that sense, since we are ultimately one with God. The lesson of the Moses Code is that we cannot be separated from truth except in our minds. Release the thought of separation, and miracles happen all around us."

"And the other Divine Names—how do they relate to all this?"

"Each aspect of God, represented by the various names of God, are aspects within each one of us. They're lessons that remind us who we are when we're aligned with the Divine within us. If we live in the ego, then we live our lives opposing the attributes of God, but when we live from our souls, then those same aspects take us over and we resonate with them on the deepest levels. I believe this is something that has always been understood and lived by the greatest mystics and saviors, such as Jesus, for example, when he used the 'I AM' so expertly. Now it's time for us to do the same, to live from a fully awakened heart and a fully realized soul, which is the source of our lives and highest nature." The words had flowed so fast from my lips that my own mind couldn't keep up with them. I had to stop and take a deep breath before I realized what I said, and how true it all felt.

"Okay." Phil smiled. "That means we're ready to go."

It was only then that I realized that the train had come to a stop, and people were making their way to the door. "Was that okay . . . what I just said?"

Phil turned back to me. "That wasn't only you speaking. It was also Eleazar."

"What do you mean?"

"It's what I've been saying all along. Eleazar has merged, or braided, with your consciousness in some way, at least for the duration of this journey. I felt it yesterday morning after you told me about your first dream."

"My *first* dream?"

"Yes, the first, and there was another last night. I already know about it. I was watching just as I did the night before. It all tells me one thing: that we're ready. And in many ways, everything has led to this one moment. I don't know what's about to happen here, but I know that it will be perfect."

A whistle sounded, indicating that we had to hurry. We grabbed our backpacks and stepped off the train.

"I can't believe this!" I exclaimed, as we stepped out from beneath the covered enclosure. In a matter of minutes, the blue sky had turned dark with clouds, and rain was beginning to pour. The wind had also begun whipping through the station, and it only increased as we stepped out into the narrow street. We opened our umbrellas and had to lean into the wind to prevent them from being torn apart.

"This is amazing," I added. "It was looking like it was going to be a beautiful day. This seems to have come out of nowhere."

I looked over at Phil, but he didn't answer. There was a look of concern on his face, and he didn't seem to be surprised or shocked at the abrupt change in weather. But he did seem worried, as if it were something he'd hoped would not occur—a sign or omen that revealed something more to him.

"Is there anything you're not telling me?" I asked as we made our way painfully down the sidewalk in the direction of the cathedral.

"No, there's nothing I'm not telling you," he stated, finally looking in my direction. "I have to say, though, that this sudden shift has me a bit worried. It could just be the weather, or it could be something more. I'm stunned that the sky darkened so fast, especially since the entire train ride was beautiful. There was hardly a cloud in sight, and the forecast for today was excellent. Let's just get to the cathedral and finish what we came here to do."

"And what is that?"

"Chant the final name and then see what happens. It's the same as yesterday. I don't want us talking ourselves into something that isn't really there, if you know what I mean. I want to sense what *is* here and then fulfill our mission."

I could see the spires in the distance, and within a minute, I saw the entire awe-inspiring structure. Even from a block away, it was an amazing sight. So much had happened here over the centuries—so many births and deaths, wars and festivals, popes and peasants who wandered down this very same street focused on the gifts this architectural giant might offer them. And now we were there, holding on to the final name as if it were a relic. *At least it wouldn't be alone,* I thought to myself. One of the most famous relics in the world lay just ahead.

"There's a shop I want to go into over there next to the cathedral," Phil said, "sells souvenirs and such. If you want to go into the crypt, you have to buy a ticket and join a guided tour. I have the feeling there's something there for us."

"Is that where they keep Mary's tunic?" I asked.

"No, that's in the main church. We can go there after the crypt."

"By the way," I said as we approached the shop. "The labyrinth is inside, isn't it? I've always heard that people come here just so they can walk—"

"Yes, that's right," Phil interrupted. "Unfortunately, it's usually completely covered with chairs, and it's difficult to get whoever is in charge to remove them. I guess they don't understand the power of walking a labyrinth."

"Does that play into what we want to accomplish here?"

"It might. Chartres is rich with opportunities, and we'll just have to wait to see what jumps out at us."

"That was just a figure of speech, right?"

Phil grinned. "Right. I don't think we have to worry about anything jumping out at us—not today." He walked inside the shop, and I followed. As I expected, it was filled with tourist mementos and gifts. I looked around as Phil tried to speak French with the woman behind the counter. In the end, they both decided it was best to stick with English.

"We're lucky," he remarked as he walked over to me. "There's a tour beginning in a few minutes, and there's only one other person signed up for it. She's French, which means the guide will need to switch back and forth as she describes things."

"That's fine. When will we be able to see the tunic?" I felt like a child who was too anxious to wait. Phil gave me a look that communicated more than words could. *Just relax and be patient,* he said with his eyes. I took a deep breath and waited for our guide to arrive.

✧✧✧

The woman placed an ancient-looking skeleton key into an even more ancient-looking keyhole. Centuries of rust and dirt forced her to use more strength than I'd expected, and seconds later, the huge door swung inward toward the dark crypt. She reached around the corner and turned a light switch, and electric fire illumined the cold stone walls. I thought about the days before electricity existed and how a guide had likely given each person a fiery torch as they entered. These and other thoughts filled my mind as the four of us entered: Phil, our guide, the unnamed French tourist, and me. Then the guide shut the door separating us from the modern world with a medieval thud. Suddenly, my mind was devoid of chatter, and I was fully present once again to the adventure at hand.

"Chartres Cathedral as we see it now was completed in 1220, but not officially dedicated until the year 1223, on the eighth of September, the birthday of the Blessed Mother," our guide stated, first in French and then English. "It is a splendid example of radiant Gothic. This area of the Beauce region—this ancient forest—has been sacred since ancient times, more ancient than the Druids. A bit later in the tour, we'll visit a place called Our Lady of the Underground."

This sparked my interest and attention. "Our Lady of the Underground?" I repeated.

"Yes, the Virgin Paritura, the Virgin who is about to give birth. If I may continue . . . at least three other cathedrals stood here on this spot before this was built. But the Middle Ages were a cruel time, and each of them fell to the various scourges of their era. Other disasters brought about varying degrees of destruction, until, of course, a local bishop decided to build one of the most glorious churches in all of Europe—the one we are standing in now. The fire of 1194, which was ignited by a lightning strike, and the French Revolution both nearly brought her to an end. But the grace of God was on her side, and she still stands as tall and proud as she ever did."

We walked through the various dark hallways and tiny chapels listening to our monotone guide describe each detail of construction and historical importance. She talked about Druids, ancient springs, healing waters, and images of virgins and children, but the fact that she spent the vast majority of her description in French made it even more difficult to hold my interest and attention. Even Phil was beginning to look impatient and agitated. I lagged behind long enough until it seemed I'd been forgotten, and then I turned back to venture off on my own.

The ancient corridors were dimly lit, and shadows made innocent sculptures seem like approaching demons. I passed through an arched entrance that led into a narrow hallway. The ceiling seemed to be lower and the hall stretched around 40 or so feet before another archway led to a different room, probably a chapel. I walked into the area and was amazed to see Templar crosses, images of the Virgin, and other strange symbols adorning almost the entire ceiling. Then I felt something familiar, almost like I was being watched, as if someone or something sleeping in the crypt had suddenly stirred and was now wide awake.

I kept walking until I passed under the second arch and found myself in a small chapel with two stained-glass windows behind the altar. The first window depicted the Sancta Camisia (Mary's tunic), and the other displayed a huge Templar cross. I wanted to shout for Phil so he could see it for himself but decided against it. I didn't want to draw too much attention or alert them to the fact that I had abandoned the small group. But it did confirm that we were in the right place and that there was something, perhaps above us in the main church, waiting patiently.

"Hello? Where are you?" It was the voice of our tour guide. My absence had been discovered, and I was forced to rejoin the others.

When the tour was over, Phil and I stood outside one of the southern entrances to the main cathedral. "Templar crosses *next to* the Sancta Camisia," I stated after I'd told Phil what I saw. "That means a lot—the fact that someone, at some point, linked the two or at least saw the influence of one over the other."

"What do you think it means?" Phil asked.

"I have no idea yet, but the answer must lie inside, so let's go see."

We entered Chartres through the west front and what is called the Royal Portal. In the tympanum of the right-hand doorway was an amazing sculpture of the Virgin and Child seated upon a throne of wisdom and flanked by angels. Phil told me that the north entrance to the basilica depicted the crowning of the Virgin, as well as her death and Assumption. He then pointed to the second window on the south ambulatory, to what is considered the finest and most beautiful example of stained glass in all the world: *Notre-Dame de la Belle Verrière*, the famous Blue Virgin Window. It shows Mary and Child in blue on the Seat of Wisdom against a red background. The window survived the fire of 1194, and its alchemical blue light has captivated millions through the centuries.

I was nearly overwhelmed with the beauty and magnificence of the cathedral, perhaps more than any other place we visited in Paris, including Notre-Dame.

Phil pointed to the middle of the nave, and just as he'd told me, I saw the famous labyrinth completely ignored beneath many rows of chairs. I walked over and stood on one of the circular pathways, walking only three steps before being blocked by a chair. It seemed a shame, but then I remembered what he said—sometimes the trick is finding your way into the labyrinth as well as the way out. We weren't there for anything other than fulfilling our mission with the final Sacred Name. All that was left was for us to find the right place, chant the name, and then wait. What happened after that was anyone's guess.

Something drew my attention to one of the side chapels to our right, the first bay of the north ambulatory. A group of people knelt and prayed while others took pictures. I wondered if it was the famous relic so many revered: the tunic that once belonged to the Blessed Mother. I walked over with Phil following close behind, but when we arrived, I realized it was something very different yet just as interesting.

"Ah, Our Lady of the Pillar, Chartres's Black Madonna," Phil stated.

"What can you tell me about the Black Madonna?" I asked. "It's something I've read about but never fully understood."

A young woman with flowing red hair was standing next to us and must have overheard the conversation. "It's always assumed that it's a statue of the Mary," she replied in a thick French accent, "the Mother of Jesus, but in these parts, there is a very different understanding. The color black refers to the one who was pushed into the background, relegated to the shadows—Mary Magdalene. As you probably know, the early church never understood her role or her relationship with Jesus, and it has little to do with whether or not she was his wife. At the very least, she was one of his confidants, if not his closest one; and even today, she's sometimes called the Apostles' Apostle.

"But the church didn't want her stealing the light, so she was turned into a prostitute and a sinner, none of which was true. Most people don't even realize that a number of years ago, the Pope issued a statement reversing the church's position on that matter, saying that there was no link between Mary Magdalene and the adulterous woman in the gospel story. Anyway, in France she was never forgotten, but she was disguised. What you're looking at here is the mask she's worn for 2,000 years—the mask of darkness."

"Is there any link with the Templars?" I inquired.

"The Templars?" She seemed surprised that I would bring them up. I was even more shocked by her answer. "It is strange that you would think to ask me that. Yes, actually there is. It's believed that St. Bernard de Clairvaux had a very strong relationship with the Black Madonna, and a historian named Ean Begg suggested that there was an esoteric branch within the Templars, which revered the Magdalene in her shadowy form. Suffice it to say that since the Templars were powerful here in France, there's little chance they could have avoided the association, and given their less than orthodox rituals and practices, it's likely that the association was deep. Does that answer your question?"

Before I could answer, she walked away, and Phil and I looked at each other.

"Did that just happen, or was she in my imagination?" I muttered.

"Best not ask questions like that in here," he replied. "Some mysteries are better left unsolved."

"I agree. We'll leave it for now."

"Have you ever heard of the concept of *Theotokos*?" Phil asked me.

"I think so. It's the doctrine that states that Mary was the Mother of God."

"Yes, it was proclaimed at the Council of Ephesus in 431. You may not know this, but the first stage in the alchemical process is called the *negrido* or 'black stage.' It's all about liberating the light in dark matter—what the alchemists called the *materia prima*. It's been said that the return of the Shekinah will finally liberate matter from its bondage. She is the liberating angel and the sum total of all the Divine Names. She is Mary, Mother of the World. This is the best way I have of describing this concept."

The dark Madonna held the Christ child in her arms, and both were clothed in magnificent gowns covered with jewels. There were also crowns atop their heads, and each of them had one hand outstretched with what looked like a single finger extended in a John the Baptist gesture. It was as if they were both pointing toward Heaven, or perhaps even indicating the number 1, which was more likely.

"Do you think this is where we should chant the last name?" I asked.

"Actually, no. Let's move a bit farther down. I want you to see something."

I looked in the direction he motioned toward and saw a larger group of people standing at another side altar. We walked in that direction, and I felt my heart beginning to stir in a familiar way—an emotion I both welcomed and desired. It reminded me of the feeling I experienced when I met the beautiful nun who was trapped inside the Church of the Assumption and the rapture I sensed at the Chapel of the Miraculous Medal when I witnessed the heavenly light enveloping the body of St. Catherine. It grew stronger as we approached, and I knew before we arrived what it meant.

Phil turned to me. "The Chapel of Saint-Piat and the veil or tunic of the Blessed Mother."

It was enshrined in a small glass case and was locked inside a golden church-shaped reliquary with two gold angels on either side. The cloth was stretched inside and didn't look at all like the 2,000 year old tunic it was said to be. The glass case sat atop a stone altar, and within seconds, I spotted something carved into it, which was directly aligned with the relic. I nudged Phil. "Do you see that? It's a Templar cross right beneath the cloth."

"Yes, of course, but I never noticed it till now."

"Everywhere we go . . . it's like bread crumbs leading us somewhere."

"I think they've led us here," Phil said, "to this Our Lady of Chartres. It's also leading us to the final Sacred Name we'll chant. This adventure began with the Moses Code and 'I AM THAT, I AM,' and now it ends there with *Ehyeh Asher Ehyeh*. Everywhere we've gone we found symbols and signs that told us we were in the right place. I don't know about you, but this feels like the last and most important of them all."

"Do you think we should do our chant here by the Sancta Camisia?"

Phil looked around as if trying to make a decision. "Yes, I think we should. If we walk over to the side, we can probably avoid the crowd."

We found a spot on the wall, and I stood facing it with my head resting against the cold stone. Phil stood a foot or two beside me, just close enough for me to hear him clearly. Then I took three deep breaths, somehow sensing that our journey was about to reach a final climax, even though I still had no idea what that really meant. Would I finally be able to grasp why Phil felt it was so important to use the Sacred Names in this way? Would I be able to rest knowing that I did what I could to understand everything that began with a simple comma, but that led to so much more? There were so many threads that seemed to be weaving themselves together. I just hoped that I'd be able to see the tapestry it created and comprehend what it was all for.

Phil began speaking. "We're going to activate the first name that God gave Moses at the burning bush through the Angel of Light. This is the name that, as you say, indicates that we are one with God and all creation. It also contains the secret for creating miracles in our lives and in the world. When we understand that God claims and accepts us this and every moment, and that we are worthy of the abundance of the Universe, then all things flow to us with ease and grace. Haven't you noticed how much *Ehyeh* sounds like *Ah, Yeah*? This is part of the secret you cracked—when we say *yes*, we invoke the full creative power of the Universe. This is the lesson of *Ehyeh Asher Ehyeh,* the Moses Code, and the lesson we learn today."

Then we began our final chant: *"Ehyeh Asher Ehyeh, En Sof; Ehyeh Asher Ehyeh, En Sof; Ehyeh Asher Ehyeh, En Sof. . . ."*

My forehead was pressed against the wall and as I tried to push away, something seemed to hold me in place. I attempted to raise my hands to gain leverage, but no matter how hard I tried, I couldn't move. Then the natural sounds of the cathedral seemed to fade, and I had the sensation that someone was standing behind me, but it wasn't Phil. I caught his silhouette as he walked away toward the Sancta Camisia, and still I felt the presence—even a shallow breath against my neck. I wanted to turn around and dispel the illusion, but my paralysis continued. I suddenly heard the sound of parting lips, as if someone were about to speak . . . and then came the words: *A great sign in Heaven; a woman clothed with the Sun, and the Moon under her feet, and upon her head a crown of 12 stars. She was pregnant and screamed in the anguish of delivery.*

Then I remembered the dream from two nights ago—the scene appearing in my mind as if I were watching a movie. Every detail was present, and although I was still completely conscious of my body pressed against the wall, I was also totally present in the memory itself. I looked in front of me and saw the woman in labor, lying in the bed as the concerned women surrounded her. The woman was screaming with pain, and I felt myself stepping forward as I had done before.

One of the women addressed me. "Please help us. She is going to die, and the baby with her. Please help her live."

Then the pregnant woman looked deep into my eyes and said, "You know what to do. It is nearly time, but I can't do this without you."

"But why me? Why do I need to be here for you to give birth?"

"You seem to be one man," she stated, "but there are so many more. And they are all here with you. Each of the names represents a different aspect of not only God, but humanity itself. And that is why you brought them here, all the names you chanted, because they would bring all the world here as well. And when you are all represented and are able to hold the energy with me, then I will be able to bring the child into the world."

"Who is the child?" I asked. "Is it an actual baby, or are you speaking about something much more esoteric?"

But before she could answer, she turned away as a contraction ripped through her body. "Do what you know how to do," the woman beside her said. "It is almost too late."

I placed my face against her belly just as I had done before and began chanting the final Sacred Name. *"Ehyeh Asher Ehyeh, En Sof; Ehyeh Asher Ehyeh, En Sof; Ehyeh Asher Ehyeh, En Sof . . ."*

My eyes were closed as I chanted the name, and I could hear the sounds of the women and their heart-wrenching weeping. Then I opened my eyes and realized that I wasn't in the same room at all—once again, I found myself in the streets of ancient Jerusalem. I wondered what was happening and then began running, looking for Eleazar. Minutes later, I saw a flight of stone steps and somehow knew that I should go to the top of the wall that enclosed the city. I ran as fast as I could, rising above the throng and the noise of the market. When I finally arrived, I covered my eyes from the sun and scanned the crowd.

"Who is it you're looking for, my son?"

I turned around and saw the rabbi standing to my left. "Rabbi—what's happening to me?" I was panting, and it took me a few seconds to catch my breath. "It's all starting to make sense, and yet it makes no sense at all."

"Ah yes, but what does make sense in a world of seeming paradoxes, my son? Truth may be the most transient and impermanent of all things. You feel the truth and know the truth, but the mind alone cannot by itself grasp its full meaning. It's like water, which is always seeking its source. The more we try and hold on to it, the more of its essence we lose. But what is lost on us is not lost on the world. It will nourish new growth elsewhere in the garden that may not have happened otherwise. Do you understand what I'm saying? There are no mistakes. Even when it seems that we are moving backward, there is an *aspect* of us that always moves forward."

"So much of this has centered on aspects," I remarked, *"aspects* of God and *aspects* of humanity. I'm realizing now that it's all the same. The names we've been using aren't just about God. They're our names as well. They're about invoking God's presence in all of us. That has to be what the dreams were about. The woman giving birth said that the Sacred Names represent all of humanity. Has that been the point of this journey from the beginning?"

"The point has been for you to play your role in the restoration of the world, beginning with yourself. Each one of us has a role to play, and this is yours. Phil told you from the very beginning that using the power contained in the names never had anything to do with anyone but *you*. It was always about your personal relationship with God—or however you choose to define the Almighty One— even when it seems to be about the whole world. We make special prayers of unification. They're called *Yihudim*. What you were both doing was not so different in essence—a sanctification of the name. I'm happy to see you're beginning to understand."

"I'm beginning to understand a lot. Everything I've experienced and learned has led to her—to the Mother."

"And who is the Mother?"

"The Mother of us all, everywhere and in all her forms. It's the Blessed Mother and Mary Magdalene. It's Ameratsu, Kuan Yin, and Demeter. It's the feminine aspect of God—the Shekinah."

"Yes, the Divine presence of God in the world. And what is she trying to say to us?"

"I think she's trying to give birth to a new world. She's in labor, and it's very difficult. She needs our help—otherwise, I believe the world will suffer greatly. The point of this whole journey seems to be helping the birth of a new world, what you might call *the world to come*."

"And where will that new world be born?" the rabbi asked me.

"Where will it be born? In each one of us, I'm thinking."

"Yes, that's true. But there's something else, another aspect as you say, and it surrounds you now in this moment. So I'll ask again. Where will this new world be born?"

I looked around and saw people walking and horses pulling carts. There were stands set up along the road with merchants selling a wide variety of vegetables, fruits, incense, and spices; and people of every race and color seemed to be present. In that instant, something seemed to click inside me, as if everything finally fell into place, and I suddenly saw what had always been right in front of me. "She'll give birth here, in Jerusalem," I declared. "That's why I keep coming back—it was right here all along."

"In your book of Revelation, is there not a description of a woman giving birth? She's clothed with the sun and the moon under her feet with a circle of 12 stars around her head. I think you've seen her before, yes?"

"I think I actually heard her," I replied. "Right after Phil and I chanted the last name, I heard a voice quote a verse from Revelation in my ear. But what does it mean?"

"You already know what it means. You said it yourself. The birth is taking place here in Jerusalem, the City of Peace. So the question is, Who is the woman? The answer is . . ."

Once again my mind reached for the answer, through all the experiences with Phil, all the entities we had encountered, and all the lessons I'd learned. The Hebrew names of God had been activated, opening gates within me, and now it was time for them to congeal into a meaningful lesson or whole, something I could understand and communicate to others—something that would impact the whole world. I was in Jerusalem again, a city I had visited many times before and where some of the most powerful peacemakers I have ever met live and work. But who was the woman giving birth here, and why would she . . . "Israel!" I exclaimed as soon as the thought entered my mind. "The woman has to be Israel, and Jerusalem is the heart of Israel. Is that correct?"

"The heart of the spiritual Israel beats in the entire assembly, or ecclesia, of this Holy Land. You believe that Israel is the woman that the book of Revelation is referring to? If that's true, then what is the meaning of the last two days and the names of God you and your friend have been using?"

"It relates because . . . well, because if the names represent the qualities or aspects of God and we are all one in God, then the integration of the names activates *our* highest potential. And that has always been the vision of Jerusalem and Israel: to be the place

205

where peace finally prevails. So Israel is the Mother and Jerusalem is her child. Am I finally getting it?"

"When the Shekinah returns from her exile in the lower worlds," Eleazar added, "and when the head of the serpent is crushed underfoot, then she will return in her white radiance and peace will reign. It's the marriage of the Bride and the Bridegroom in Jerusalem, the City of Peace. You do know that this is what the word *Jerusalem* means, yes? And you believe that the time is now, and the place is here?"

I didn't want to answer too quickly, as if everything depended on what I said. But it felt so right, so perfect, and I knew that everything led to this one realization.

"Yes, I do believe it. I've been to Israel many times and have always felt that it was ground zero for true and lasting peace, in spite of all the violence and hatred. It always felt like it was just beneath the surface, and all it needed was the right catalyst to make it come alive."

Eleazar smiled. "And now you have brought your catalyst. Or perhaps it brought you. Either way, now you realize why the names of God are so important because they are the names of each one of us. We carry all the Sacred Names of God within us—Hebrew, Arabic, Sanskrit. They tell us that by our very nature we are Divine Creations, regardless of where we are from or how we worship. And this is where it will happen. More and more people, released of their shadows, will return to the Holy Land, to this city, and will lend their light to a flame that is already burning bright. And when it grows to the point where it can't be dimmed, then peace will prevail here and in the world."

"Is there anything else that I need to learn, Rabbi? Now that we've come to the tenth location, is there anything that's still left?"

"Only one thing," he said as he placed his hand softly on my shoulder. "Only love. This isn't about the mind or the intellect. It's about opening the heart to the love that is our very foundation. It's about opening to God's bountiful love and grace, which is our birthright as perfect children of God. When you do that, everything you have learned will occur on its own. You won't need to do anything except watch in amazement."

I closed my eyes to feel it as deeply as possible. "I am amazed. I'm amazed that it's so simple and so elegant . . ."

✧✧✧

"What's so simple?" My eyes were still closed, and I was jarred by the question. "Jimmy, what's so simple?"

I opened my eyes to see that I was still in the cathedral with Phil at my side. He had his hand on my shoulder and a concerned look on his face. "Simple?" I asked, shaking my head a bit to readjust. "How long have I been standing here?"

"We just finished chanting the final name. I walked away for about a minute and then saw you speaking to yourself, so I thought I should stay close. You were starting to get a bit loud, and people were beginning to look. I figured it was time to do something."

"I was talking to myself?" I asked, still a bit shaky from the shift. "No, I was with Eleazar in Jerusalem, and now I understand what this is all about."

"Tell me everything."

We walked to the back of the church and sat down in one of the chairs. I told him about finding the rabbi and everything he shared with me. Then I described my realization regarding Israel and the destiny of Jerusalem in particular. He seemed to like what he heard and nodded his head as I spoke.

"What do you think about all that?" I asked him when I finished.

"It's what I suspected all along. Everything has led us back to the Mother from the very beginning. And why not? It's what this time is all about. And of course it all comes back to Jerusalem, a city you've embraced for so long. A city that keeps calling you back."

"That's the answer to the code, then," I remarked. "It was her, the Divine Feminine. She's the one who led us on this journey from the beginning."

"It was a journey that could only lead to one place," Phil maintained, as if he himself understood what I was thinking and feeling on a deeper level. "It could only lead back to the heart. And that being said, I was wondering if you noticed where we're sitting?"

I glanced around but didn't notice anything out of the ordinary. "Look down," Phil said.

I looked down and realized that the chairs we sat in were in the very middle of the Chartres Labyrinth—its heart, the heart of the entire cathedral, that was dedicated to Mary, the Mother of the Universe. Every twist and turn we had experienced on our journey had led us here, to the center of everything sacred. It was the perfect ending to two of the most powerful days of my life.

"Where do we go from here?"

Phil smiled. "Now we live it. We knew from the first name that this wasn't about anything other than opening our hearts to a greater truth, and in the process, a higher love. Now that we've achieved this, we must share it. That's how the destiny of Jerusalem and the re-creation of the world will be realized. *It's through each one of us living the Sacred Names in our everyday lives.* Incidentally, did you know that the labyrinth used to be called the 'Jerusalem Way'?"

I took hold of his arm and stood up from the chair. "That's all I needed to hear. I think I finally get what this was all about."

The End

✧✧✧✧✧

Afterword
by Phil Gruber

"It was my destiny to join in a great experience."
— from *The Journey to the East* by Herman Hesse

When James Twyman contacted me about joining him in Switzerland in early April 2008, I had no idea at the time that, just beyond the veil, an adventure was being rehearsed for us that would come to be the inspiration for this book. I had been recuperating at my sister's home from a bout of depression, and I wasn't sure that traveling was such a good idea. But James seemed very keen to have me along as a support and friend, and I was happy to oblige. As he states early on in the book, after the confrontation with the audience member at *The Moses Code* movie premiere, he truly wanted to learn more about the Yud. It was an invitation I could hardly turn down.

Peace Troubadour is a role that James was born to play. He has been one of my closest friends for many years, and I've always believed that the idea of setting the 12 peace prayers from the major religions of the world to music was seeking him out. They were known as "The Peace Seeds" and had been prayed in Assisi, Italy, in 1986 by the leaders of each religion. Jimmy already had the music inside of him, and through him, the prayers found their voice. Because of his teachings and music, many thousands around the world have found their song, their paths are more brightly illuminated, and their destinies have been brought more clearly into focus as a result of his love and tireless work as a peacemaker.

In the interests of space, we couldn't fully document all of the miracles that occurred during our time in Paris. For me, the journey was a love letter written in the language of birds, branches, and stone. It was an adventure of a lifetime . . . ah, springtime in Paris! Maybe it's time for the Yud to extend an *aleph branch* so the *hidden one* can finally come out of hiding, and beginning and ending can once again be joined. Who was it who said that "the closer the source, the purer the stream"?

Beyond the veils of negative existence in the house of treasures, there is a Torah yet to be revealed. I hope we're all on hand for the unveiling! Thank you, Jimmy.

"Wo [sic] unto the man who asserts that this Torah intends to relate only commonplace things and secular narratives; for if this were so, then in the present times likewise a Torah might be written with more attractive narratives. . . . Now the narratives of the Torah are its garments. He who thinks that these garments are the Torah itself deserve to perish and have no share in the world to come. Woe onto the fools who look no further when they see an elegant robe! More valuable even than that is the soul which animates the body. Fools see only the garment of the Torah, the more intelligent see the body, the wise see the soul, its proper being; and in the Messianic time the 'upper soul' of the Torah will stand revealed."
— *Zohar*, iii. 152, as quoted by Louis Ginzberg in
On Jewish Law and Lore

Bibliography

The Bahir. Ed. and Trans. Aryeh Kaplan. New York: Samuel Weiser, 1979.

Bardon, Franz. *The Key to the True Kabbalah.* Trans. Gerhard Hanswille. Salt Lake City: Merkur Publishing, Inc., 2002.

Bar-Lev, Rabbi Yechiel. *Song of the Soul: Introduction to Kaballa.* Israel: Petach Tikva, 1994.

Berg, Philip S. *Kabbalah for the Layman: A Guide to Cosmic Consciousness, Volume I.* Jerusalem: Research Center of Kabbalah, 1988.

Berg, Yehuda. *The Power of Kabbalah.* San Diego: Jodere Group, Inc., 2001.

Blumenthal, David R. *Understanding Jewish Mysticism.* New York: Ktav, 1978.

Carroll, Lewis. *Through the Looking-Glass and What Alice Found There: With Fifty Illustrations.* Charleston, SC: BookSurge, 2001.

Crowley, Aleister. *Magick: Liber Aba: Book 4.* York Beach, MA: Weiser Books, 1980.

DuQuette, Lon Milo. *Enochian Vision Magick: An Introduction and Practical Guide to the Magick of Dr. John Dee and Edward Kelley.* San Francisco: Weiser, 2008.

Eco, Umberto. *Foucault's Pendulum.* Ballantine Books, 1990.

Eisen, William. *The Universal Language of Cabalah.* Camarillo, CA: De Vorss & Co., 1989.

Fulcanelli. *Le Mystère des Cathédrales.* Trans. Mary Sworder. Las Vegas: Brotherhood of Life, 1990.

Gikatilla, Joseph. *Sha'are Orah: Gates of Light.* San Francisco: HarperCollins, 1994.

Ginzberg, Louis. *On Jewish Law and Lore.* Philadelphia: Jewish Publications Society of America, 1962.

Grant, Kenneth. *Outside the Circles of Time.* London: Starfire Ltd., 2007.

Hesse, Herman. *The Journey to the East.* Berlin: Samuel Fischer, 1932.

Hieronimus, J. Zohara Meyerhoff. *Kabbalistic Teachings of the Female Prophets: The Seven Holy Women of Ancient Israel.* Rochester, VT: Inner Traditions, 2008.

Hurtak, J. J. *The Book of Knowledge: The Keys of Enoch.* Los Gatos, CA: The Academy For Future Science, 1977.

————. *The Seventy-two Sacred Names of the Myriad Expressions of the Living God.* Los Gatos, CA: The Academy For Future Science, 1997.

The Kabbalah Unveiled. Trans. S. L. MacGregor Mathers. London: Kegan Paul, Trench, Trubner, 1926.

Kaplan, Aryeh. *Handbook of Jewish Thought.* New York: Moznaim, 1979.

————. *Meditation and Kabbalah.* New York: Samuel Weiser, 1978.

Leet, Leonora. *Renewing the Covenant: A Kabbalistic Guide to Jewish Spirituality.* Rochester, VT: Inner Traditions, 1999.

————. *The Secret Doctrine of Kabbalah.* Rochester, VT: Inner Traditions, 1999.

Maimonides, Moses. *The Guide for the Perplexed.* Translated from the original and annontated by M. Friedlaender. London: Trubner, 1885.

Markale, Jean. *Cathedral of the Black Madonna: The Druids and the Mysteries of Chartres.* Rochester, VT: Inner Traditions, 2004.

Munk, Michael L. *The Wisdom in the Hebrew Alphabet.* Brooklyn: Mesorah Publications Ltd., 1983.

Patai, Raphael. *The Hebrew Goddess.* 3rd enlarged ed. Detroit: Wayne State University Press, 1990.

————. *The Jewish Alchemists.* Princeton, NJ: Princeton University Press, 1994.

Querido, René M. *The Golden Age of Chartres: The Teachings of a Mystery School and the Eternal Feminine*. Fair Oaks, CA: Rudolph Steiner College Press, 2008.

Rahn, Otto. *Crusade Against the Grail: The Struggle Between the Cathars, the Templars, and the Church of Rome*. Trans. Christopher Jones. Rochester, VT: Inner Traditions, 2006.

Scholem, Gershom. *Kabbalah*. New York: New American Library, 1978.

————. *Major Trends in Jewish Mysticism*. New York: Schocken Books, 1961.

————. *On the Kabbalah and Its Symbolism*. New York: Schocken Books, 1969.

Schwartz, Howard. *Reimagining the Bible*. New York: Oxford University Press, 1998.

Smith, Edward Reaugh. *The Burning Bush*. Fair Oaks, CA: Rudolph Steiner College Press, 1997.

Suarès, Carlo. *The Cipher of Genesis: Using the Qabalistic Code to Interpret the First Book of the Bible and the Teachings of Jesus*. Intro. Gregg Braden. Boston, MA: Weiser Books, 2005.

————. *The Sepher Yetsira*. Trans. Micheline and Vincent Stuart. Boulder: Shambhala, 1976.

Szekely, Edmond Bordeaux. Editor and Translator. *The Essene Gospel of Peace, Book Two*. Costa Rica: International Biogenic Society, 1977.

Tyson, Donald. *Tetragrammaton: The Secret to Evoking Angelic Powers and the Key to the Apocalypse*. St. Paul, MN: Llewellyn Publications, 1995.

Waite, A. E. *The Holy Kabbalah*. New Hyde Park, NY: University Books, 1969.

Wasserman, James. *The Templars and the Assassins: The Militia of Heaven*. Rochester, VT: Destiny Books, 2001.

The Zohar. Pritzker Edition. Trans. with commentary by Daniel C. Matt. Stanford, CA: Stanford University Press, 2003.

Acknowledgments

From James:

Most of all, I would like to thank Phil Gruber for his insights, wisdom, and willingness to be part of this grand adventure. It was a profound treat. Thanks also to Aurora Pagonis, my dear friend and someone who offered great support and assistance. She was actually with us on a large part of this journey but was not included in the story. Thank you for continuing to show up in such unselfish ways. I also want to thank Swami Swaroopananda for his help and support, as well as everyone at the Paradise Island Sivananda Yoga Ashram. Never stop inviting me back, please. Finally, thanks to everyone at Hay House, especially Reid Tracy and Jill Kramer. Your support means the world to me.

✧✧✧

From Phil:

I would like to thank all the great teachers, sages, Kabbalists, and Merkubalim of blessed memory; Rabbis Isaac Luria, the "Ari," and the whole Circle of Safed, Abba, Aaron Berekiah ben Moses, Chaim and Shmuel Vital, Moses de Leon, Schomo Alkabetz, Abulafia, Shalom Sharabi, Shimon bar Yohai, Moses Cordovero, Akiva, Ben Azzai, Israel Baal-Shem Tov, Nahmanides, Moses Maimonides, Nachman, Abraham ben Mordechai Azulai, Ashlag, Joseph Caro, Moses Luzzato, and so many more.

Special thanks to Laurie Rosenfield of the Spiritual Center in Toronto for her love, support, wisdom, and encouragement; Howard Schwartz, Jean Markale, my old teacher Fulcanelli, Drs. J.J. and Desiree Hurtak, friends of the AFFS worldwide, Lon Milo Duquette, James Wasserman, Linda Russell, Roland Trandafir wherever you are, Wikipedia, Donald Tyson, Helene of Montmartre, Bergs Karen, Philip S., Yehuda, and Michael. And to everyone at Kabbalah Centers east and west; the Beloved Community; Ministers of Spiritual Peacemaking; Lenore; A.D.; my lovely wife, Sharmiila; my mother, Estelle, who still doesn't understand a word I say; my sister, Paula; all my teachers past, present, and future; and Madonna, who crossed the millennium on a Ray of Light.

✧✧✧✧✧

About the Authors

James F. Twyman is the best-selling author of ten books, including *The Moses Code, Emissary of Light,* and *The Art of Spiritual Peacemaking.* He's also an internationally renowned "Peace Troubadour" who has the reputation for drawing millions of people together in prayer to positively influence crises throughout the world. He has been invited by leaders of countries such as Iraq, Northern Ireland, South Africa, Bosnia, Croatia, and Serbia to perform The Peace Concert—often while conflicts raged in those areas; and he has performed at the United Nations, the Pentagon, and more. James is the executive producer and co-writer of the feature film *Indigo,* and the director of *Indigo Evolution* and the documentary *The Moses Code.* He is also a member of the Order of St. Francis and the co-director of the World Community of Saint Francis.

Websites: **www.themosescode.com** or
www.jamestwyman.com

ﾟﾟﾟ

Phil Gruber's passion, kind spirit, and sparkling wit have made him a much-loved and highly respected speaker on the international scene. He lectures worldwide on a variety of subjects and has spoken at the United Nations. Phil resides in Melbourne, Australia, with his wife, Sharmiila.

Website: **www.philgruber.com**

Notes

Notes

Notes

Notes

Notes

Notes

Hay House Titles of Related Interest

YOU CAN HEAL YOUR LIFE, the movie,
starring Louise L. Hay & Friends
(available as a 1-DVD program and an expanded 2-DVD set)
Watch the trailer at: **www.LouiseHayMovie.com**

THE SHIFT, the movie,
starring Dr. Wayne W. Dyer
(available as a 1-DVD program and an expanded 2-DVD set)
Watch the trailer at: **www.DyerMovie.com**

✷✷✷

THE AMAZING POWER OF DELIBERATE INTENT:
Living the Art of Allowing, by Esther and Jerry Hicks
(The Teachings of Abraham®)

THE BIOLOGY OF BELIEF: *Unleashing the Power of
Consciousness, Matter & Miracles,* by Bruce H. Lipton, Ph.D.

THE DIVINE MATRIX: *Bridging Time, Space, Miracles, and Belief,*
by Gregg Braden

MESSAGES FROM SPIRIT: *The Extraordinary Power of Oracles,
Omens, and Signs,* by Colette Baron-Reid

SECRET SOCIETIES . . . *and How They Affect Our Lives Today,*
by Sylvia Browne

SOLOMON'S ANGELS: *Ancient Secrets of Love, Manifestation,
Power, Wisdom, and Self-Confidence,* by Doreen Virtue

THE SPONTANEOUS HEALING OF BELIEF:
Shattering the Paradigm of False Limits, by Gregg Braden

All of the above are available at your local bookstore,
or may be ordered by contacting Hay House (see last page).

✷✷✷

✧✧✧

We hope you enjoyed this Hay House book. If you'd like to receive
a free catalog featuring additional Hay House books and products, or
if you'd like information about the Hay Foundation, please contact:

Hay House, Inc.
P.O. Box 5100
Carlsbad, CA 92018-5100

(760) 431-7695 or (800) 654-5126
(760) 431-6948 (fax) or (800) 650-5115 (fax)
www.hayhouse.com® • www.hayfoundation.org

✧✧✧

Published and distributed in Australia by: Hay House Australia Pty.
Ltd., 18/36 Ralph St., Alexandria NSW 2015 • *Phone:* 612-9669-4299
Fax: 612-9669-4144 • www.hayhouse.com.au

Published and distributed in the United Kingdom by:
Hay House UK, Ltd., 292B Kensal Rd., London W10 5BE
Phone: 44-20-8962-1230 • *Fax:* 44-20-8962-1239 • www.hayhouse.co.uk

Published and distributed in the Republic of South Africa by:
Hay House SA (Pty), Ltd., P.O. Box 990, Witkoppen 2068 • *Phone/Fax:*
27-11-467-8904 • orders@psdprom.co.za • www.hayhouse.co.za

Published in India by: Hay House Publishers India,
Muskaan Complex, Plot No. 3, B-2, Vasant Kunj, New Delhi 110 070
Phone: 91-11-4176-1620 • *Fax:* 91-11-4176-1630 • www.hayhouse.co.in

Distributed in Canada by: Raincoast,
9050 Shaughnessy St., Vancouver, B.C. V6P 6E5
Phone: (604) 323-7100 • *Fax:* (604) 323-2600 • www.raincoast.com

✧✧✧

Tune in to **HayHouseRadio.com®** for the best in inspirational talk
radio featuring top Hay House authors! And, sign up via the Hay
House USA Website to receive the Hay House online newsletter and
stay informed about what's going on with your favorite authors. You'll
receive bimonthly announcements about Discounts and Offers, Special
Events, Product Highlights, Free Excerpts, Giveaways, and more!
www.hayhouse.com®

To:

HAY HOUSE, INC.
P.O. Box 5100
Carlsbad, CA 92018-5100

Tune in to Hay House Radio to listen to your favorite authors: **HayHouseRadio.com**™

Yes, I'd like to receive:

☐ ☐ **a Hay House catalog** ☐ ☐ *The Louise Hay Newsletter*
The Christiane Northrup Newsletter *The Sylvia Browne Newsletter*

Name_____

Address_____

City_____ State _____ Zip _____

E-mail_____

Also, please send:

☐ ☐ **a Hay House catalog** ☐ ☐ *The Louise Hay Newsletter*
The Christiane Northrup Newsletter *The Sylvia Browne Newsletter*

To:
Name_____

Address_____

City_____ State _____ Zip _____

E-mail_____

If you'd like to receive a catalog of Hay House books and products, or a free copy of one or more of our authors' newsletters, please visit **www.hayhouse.com**® or detach and mail this reply card.